WomanWord

OTHER PUBLICATIONS
BY THE AUTHOR

Books

Preparing the Way of the Lord
God-With-Us: Resources for Prayer and Praise
Why Sing? Toward A Theology of Catholic Church Music
An Anthology of Scripture Songs
WomanPrayer, WomanSong: Resources for Ritual

Records/Cassettes/Published Music Collections

Joy Is Like the Rain
I Know the Secret
Knock, Knock
Seasons
Gold, Incense, and Myrrh
In Love
Mass of a Pilgrim People
RSVP: Let Us Pray
Songs of Promise
Sandstone
Remember Me
WomanSong

Music resources are available from Medical Mission Sisters
77 Sherman Street/Hartford, CT 06105/203-233-0875/203-232-4451

WomanWord

A Feminist Lectionary
and Psalter

Women of the New Testament

Miriam Therese Winter

Illustrated by Meinrad Craighead

CROSSROAD • NEW YORK

1994

The Crossroad Publishing Company
370 Lexington Avenue, New York, NY 10017

Printed in the United States of America
Typesetting output: TEXSource, Houston

Cover illustration and text illustrations: Meinrad Craighead

Library of Congress Cataloging-in-Publication Data

Winter, Miriam Therese.
    Womanword : a feminist lectionary and psalter : women of the New Testament / Miriam Therese Winter ; illustrated by Meinrad Craighead.
    p. cm.
   ISBN: 0-8245-1054-2 (pbk.)
    1. Women in the Bible. 2. Women—Prayer-books and devotions—English. 3. Bible. N.T.—Devotional literature. I. Title.
BS2445.W55 1990
264'.13'082—dc20   90-37970
                                                                CIP

Contents

III ◇ WOMEN AND THE SPIRIT OF JESUS AND SHADDAI

◇ SONGS ◇

Psalms

PREFACE

To MAKE RITUAL IS TO REMEMBER INTO LIFE AND INTO MEANING, to determine who and what will survive from generation to generation, what people will be honored, what values will be strengthened, what traditions are worth keeping, what perspectives will be handed on.

Religion's selective memory ordinarily eliminates the losers and disdains the common touch. Rites rehearse the victories that theology supports and embellishes, structures maintain and perpetuate, and canons guarantee. Only institutional myths are deemed authoritative, only canonical images and symbols are accorded legitimacy.

Ritual not only transmits perspective, it also molds reality according to its worldview. Women have come to realize that the worldview by which they must live, move, and struggle into freedom is held firmly in place by a history of ritual conditioned by male perceptions and male interpretations. Paradigms of faith and fidelity are rooted in male experience. Images and symbols reflect and reinforce a patriarchal bias. Rites and ritual behavior are determined by the men who are in control. True gender mutuality will not occur until the fundamental assumptions at the heart of our religious ritual undergo a radical change. When that which is liturgically rehearsed is no longer the way men want the world to be but the way it should and could be, then the whole of humanity, female and male, will know a heartfelt liberation and the world will take one giant step toward realizing the reign of God.

Authentic religious ritual invites a person into community and that community into worship. It holds up for collective encouragement ordinary people as heroines and heroes and retells their stories in a way that helps us to focus on our own. In the spirit of Jesus authentic Christian ritual seeks inspiration from the underside of tradition, sees prophets among the outcasts, sings songs that arise from the margins, offers prayers culturally conditioned by a minority point of view. Religious ritual that is relevant and flexible prepares a pathway into the mysteries of the God Who is beyond us and yet within us. In so doing, it does not stifle initiative but rather rejoices when individuals, responsive to the Spirit, share wisdom for the common good. Naming God and proclaiming God is an enterprise of freedom. There is a sense of belonging and a love of diversity.

Any ritual that consistently excludes a culture, a gender, or a legitimate tradition and claims for itself the whole of truth does not speak for God. Too much of our traditional ritual is caught up in exorbitant claims that promise far more than they can deliver. That is not to say that there is no place for the established rites of our religions. It is simply to question what the rites intend and for whom they are intended. When the worldview of rites no longer coincides with the worldview of their ritual makers, something has got to change.

Women today long for authentic ritual, for liturgies that touch upon their inner truth and support their search for integration with the world of their experience. Women want rituals that take seriously their innate hunger for meaning, their cry for systemic justice, and their need to dwell in God. They want to hear about other women's struggles to keep and transmit the faith. They seek a sense of solidarity with sister saints and sister sinners, with those women who were touched by Jesus, who were caught up in the Spirit, who nurtured the newborn church when there was still a chance to shape its identity in the inclusive image of God.

In their search for female predecessors, women have found that most of their story has simply disappeared. Women are rarely featured in the New Testament scriptures. When they are, they are seldom named. Their experience is distorted, their contributions deleted, their status so diminished that one may well conclude that their lives are irretrievably lost.

Women's reality has also been minimized in the church's lectionary. Readings throughout the liturgical year either ignore women or present a portion of their narrative out of context. Even well-intentioned celebrants fail to represent the truth of women's experience, and more often than not misinterpret their importance in the life and mission of Jesus as well as their impact on the early church. Consequently, a growing number of women have begun to imaginatively reconstruct the lost lives of their invisible sisters, convinced that the biblical tradition is far more inclusive of women than the received texts might imply. In addition, women are liturgically chastised from time to time through lections that focus on outmoded behavior. Such androcentric texts favor the perpetuation of past practice more than the proclamation of a healing word for all God's wounded daughters. Feminist biblical scholars have dared to suggest that biblical texts supporting anything less than the full liberation of women are not to be considered Gospel, for authoritative revelation is a liberating word.

Women wait to hear Good News through the words and the lives of women, hoping to release female leaders and liturgical pioneers from the anonymity of the past to serve as role models for the present.

WomanWord came into being in response to these concerns. It was born of a strong conviction: before we consider what is not in the scriptures, we first need to know what is there. We need to know and remember. Who were the women with Jesus? Who were the women who were present during the birthpangs of the church? We need to tell their stories. We need to remember their names.

We remember best through ritual. *WomanWord* is a book for ritual, a lectionary containing the life stories of all those women whose historical existence has been recorded in the New Testament canon. For some there is very little information beyond a greeting and a name. Others are described more fully yet remain anonymous. All of the scriptures pertaining to each woman comprise that woman's story, so that all that is presently known of these women, and some of what has been said about them, has been included here.

The number of New Testament women who speak through *WomanWord* is cause for some surprise. There are forty-eight separate entries with a total of sixty-four women individually identified. Texts that refer to groups of women indicate that many more were involved in the life and ministry of Jesus and in those early Christian initiatives that followed upon Pentecost. The narratives in *WomanWord* represent a broad spectrum of womanhood: mothers, wives, and widows, sisters and daughters, prophets, a slave, young and old, rich and poor, in-laws and outcasts, prostitutes and virgins, princesses and servants, sinners and saints, women in need of healing, women of prominence, a business woman, and quite a few women in ministry who were leaders in the church. There is even a woman named Dorcas who was brought back from the dead. We meet women at the heart of decisive events foundational to the Christian faith, at the birth, death, and resurrection of Jesus and in the upper room at Pentecost. This is Good News indeed for women and a blessing for us all.

This lectionary affirms that the God of the Hebrew scriptures is also the God of Christianity, that the Spirit of Jesus is the same Spirit of the creation narratives. Except for inclusive language and at times a female name for God, the lections relate each woman's story as it has been recorded in scripture, remembering her into the present in a simple liturgical setting with opportunity for shared reflection, a psalm response, and prayer. Some exegetical material assists our understanding of the narrative and its context. Visual portraits give form and flesh to biographical facts, and poetic reflections add a perspective of immediacy and integration. The presentation of Mary's story differs somewhat from the others. It is set within a feminist frame in order to make Mary more meaningful and more accessible to women today. The format of each entry is that of a liturgy of the word. For a more developed ritual, add your own prayers, songs, silence, dance, and other celebrational elements, or open and close your ritual with a song from the back of the book.

WomanWord takes all the received texts pertaining to historical New Testament women and sets them in a style especially suited for oral proclamation. Under Points for Shared Reflection, which can serve as a guide for personal or shared reflection, group discussion, Bible study, or the development of a homily or sermon, questions are asked of the text and its context. These points are meant to be catalytic, evoking discussion as well as further questions from ritual participants.

Women are particularly encouraged to critique the narratives in light of their own experience, applying what Elisabeth Schüssler Fiorenza calls a hermeneutics of suspicion, questioning the facts in light of feelings, filling in the missing pieces by imaginatively recreating herstory from a woman's point of view. Since all scripture is the product of male transmission, it is essential that women bring such feminist perspectives to their consideration of biblical texts. Implicit in this approach is the understanding that biblical tradition encompasses far more than what has been communicated through scripture. The narratives pertaining to women reveal inconsistencies and glaring omissions, and occasionally contradictions, as in the Resurrection narratives concerning women and the tomb. There are also larger questions. Why is it that male apostles from the time of

Jesus figure prominently in the accounts of the early church, while women of the Gospels are replaced by a whole new cast of female characters after Pentecost? How could Mary Magdalene, Mary and Martha of Bethany, and all those women healed by Jesus simply have disappeared? It is all the more amazing when we stop to recall that barely two months separate the Resurrection from Pentecost.

Such discontinuity is deceptive, and women are calling into question both theological and ritual developments based on conclusions drawn from such a selective chronicling of their lives. Although textual transmission of women's reality is both inadequate and inaccurate, women know intuitively and textual evidence confirms that women have always held a significant place in the plan of God. It remains for women to claim their place in the past and in the present. *WomanWord* offers a biblical basis for feminist hagiography. As we celebrate sisterhood, name our saints, give birth to our own psalter, we discover that the whole of our tradition is more than the sum of its segmented parts.

What a wealth of womanwisdom is yet to be found in the word of God. Feminist liturgies in the spirit of the biblical tradition celebrate a wholistic understanding of God's liberating word. Sophia, Wisdom's word, refuses to be limited either to texts or interpretations. Her word exists before, behind, beyond all words as life force in the beginning, and now, and ever after, a word empowering the powerless through liberating experiences shared and shaped through centuries of oral transmission, a word of hope for all who hunger for freedom and justice now.

The experiences of so many women, in North America, in Australia, in Cambodia, in Ghana, Kenya, and Uganda, and a concern for women everywhere gave impetus to this book. Their spirit inhabits and energizes the poems, prayers, and psalms.

I am especially grateful to three individuals for the realization of *WomanWord*. Thank you, Meinrad Craighead, for your visual words and your vision, gifts that have given our biblical sisters their visibility. You have enriched our world. Thank you, John Eagleson, for being the kind of editor of which every writer dreams. And thank you, Mary Elizabeth Johnson, for being for me the one who supports and affirms both word and song.

——— ◇ ———

◇ A PSALM ON THE WATERS OF LIFE ◇

Choir 1   Women bear
the waters of life.

Choir 2   We carry creation's waters
deep within our hallowed hollows,

Choir 1   splash, wash, refresh
the finite form that floats content
within the womb-life of the not-yet
and the womb-love of our being,

Choir 2   where a wellspring feeds, protects, rocks
the next best hope of our universe,

All   for future leaders of the world
all sail the seas within us
before they know their names.

Choir 1   Yes, long before men lay their claims
to power and opportunity,

Choir 2   all suck at our succulence
helplessly,

All   and we give of our substance
generously.

Choir 1   We women carry the waters of life
in our memory and our meaning,

Choir 2   giving heart-space, soul-space,
Spirit-space
to the circle cast
'round that sacred place
called female
deep within us.

Choir 1   Holy the healing waters.

Choir 2   Holy our sisters, mothers, daughters.

All   Holy the wisdom woman brings
to life
from hidden
hallowed springs.

By M. T. Winter, Crossroad Pub. Co., © 1990 Medical Mission Sisters   *WomanWord* / **XV**

◇ I ◇
Women and Shaddai
in the Spirit
of Jesus

ELIZABETH

◇ **Scripture Reference**   Luke 1:5–80

Elizabeth, whose name means "God has sworn [to protect us]" — it was the name of Aaron's wife — was of priestly descent and a relative of Mary the mother of Jesus. She was married to Zechariah (meaning "Yahweh has remembered"), a priest descended from Abijah, one of the twenty-four grandsons of Aaron the first high priest. Childless into old age, Elizabeth gave birth to a son, John (meaning "God is gracious"), through a miraculous intervention, long after the onset of menopause. Her child, John the baptizer, grew up to be the prophet who prepared the way for the promised Messiah.

◇ **Context**

Elizabeth's story stands at the very beginning of Luke's Gospel and unfolds in counterpoint to Mary's story. The joining of both stories, women's stories whose central theme is the salvation and liberation of all people, occurs through the deliberate intervention of God Who weaves a storyline through women's wombs against all human odds. The juxtaposition of age and youth, sterility and potential fertility, is taken up in the canticle of praise that Luke puts on the lips of Mary when the two pregnant women meet. An ancient and tenacious tradition ascribes this Magnificat originally to Elizabeth on whose lips the opening lines, derived from the song of Hannah who was also old and barren, seem especially appropriate. Because the stories of Elizabeth and Mary are so tightly interwoven, sections of the text have been repeated in the lectionary readings for both women.

◇ **Lectionary Reading**

Narrator   In the days of Herod,
king of Judea,
there lived a priest named Zechariah,
a descendant of Abijah,
who had a wife descended
from the daughters of Aaron.
Her name was Elizabeth.
Both were blameless in the eyes of God,
for they carefully kept
the commandments of God
and the observances of the Law.
But they were childless,
for Elizabeth was barren,
and now both were well advanced in years.

The First Annunciation

Zechariah was serving as priest
in the temple
when he was chosen by lot

to enter the sanctuary
and burn incense on behalf of the people
while the congregation prayed outside.
As he entered the sanctuary
an angel appeared
to the right of the altar of incense,
and Zechariah was terrified.
The angel said to him,

Angel "Do not be afraid, Zechariah,
I have come to tell you
your prayers have been heard.
Your wife Elizabeth
will bear you a son
and you shall name him John.
And you shall have joy and gladness,
and many will rejoice at his birth,
for he will grow great
in the sight of God.
He must drink no wine, no alcohol.
The Holy Spirit will permeate him,
even from his mother's womb.
Through him many of the children of Israel
will return again to God.
In the spirit and power of Elijah,
he will reconcile parents and children,
the disobedient with the wisdom
of the virtuous.
He will prepare
the people.
He will make them ready
for God."

Narrator Zechariah asked the angel,

Zechariah "How can this be, for I am old,
and my wife is well advanced in years."

Angel "I am Gabriel!
I stand in the presence of God!
I have been sent to speak to you
and to give you this good news.
Now because you did not believe my words
which will all come true in time,
you will be silent, unable to speak,
until all of this has happened."

Narrator Now the people waiting for Zechariah
were getting restless at his delay.

When he finally emerged from the sanctuary,
he could not speak to them.
As he made signs they realized
that he had seen a vision,
and the experience had left him mute.
So when his time of service ended,
Zechariah returned to his home.
Elizabeth conceived,
and for five months
she lived quietly focused within herself,
reflecting in her confinement,

Elizabeth   "God Shaddai has done this for me,
for it has pleased Her to take away
the humiliation I have suffered."

The Second Annunciation

Narrator   In the sixth month of Elizabeth's pregnancy,
the angel Gabriel appeared again,
sent by God to the Galilean town of Nazareth,
to a virgin betrothed to a man named Joseph.
The virgin's name was Mary.
The angel said to Mary:

Angel   "Rejoice, O highly favored one,
for God Shaddai is with you!"

Narrator   She was deeply disturbed by these words
and wondered what they might mean.
The angel said to her,

Angel   "Mary, do not be afraid,
for God is pleased with you.
Listen closely,
you will conceive and bear a child,
and you shall name him Jesus.
He will be great
and he will be called
the Child of God Most High.
And God will give to him
the throne of his heritage;
he will reign over all God's people,
and his reign will have no end."

Narrator   Mary said to the angel:

Mary   "How will this happen,
for I am a virgin."

Angel   "The Holy Spirit will come to you,
the shadow of Shaddai will cover you;

the child you bear will be holy
and will be called the Child of God.
Furthermore, your kinswoman Elizabeth
in her old age
has also conceived a son,
and she who was said to be barren
is already six months pregnant,
for nothing is impossible for God."

Narrator   And Mary quietly responded,

Mary   "I am one with the will of God,
let it happen as you say."

The Visitation

Narrator   Soon after,
Mary left her village
and hurried through the hills of Judea
to Elizabeth and Zechariah's home.
When Elizabeth heard Mary's greeting,
her baby leaped in her womb.
Filled with the Holy Spirit,
she cried:

Elizabeth   "Blessed are you among women,
and blessed is the child in your womb!
How can this be,
that the mother of my God
has come to visit me!
The moment your greeting
reached my ears,
my baby leaped for joy.
Blessed are you
who dared to believe
God's promise to you
would come true."

Narrator   Then they sang this song of praise:

———— ◇ ————

◇ A WOMANPSALM OF PRAISE ◇

Mary	My soul proclaims the power of God,
Elizabeth	my spirit rejoices in Shekinah/Shaddai, for She has had pity on my barrenness.
Mary	Now every generation will call me blessed, for Shaddai has done great things through me.
Both	Holy is Her name!
Mary	Her mercy extends to God-fearing people of every generation.
Elizabeth	She overwhelms the arrogant with the strength of Her outstretched arm,
Mary	putting down principalities and powers, as She gently empowers the poor.
Elizabeth	She generously feeds the hungry, and turns the wealthy away,
Mary	encouraging all who turn to Her to remember Her mercies past.
Elizabeth	She spoke through our mothers and grandmothers,
Mary	through Sarah and all her daughters who sing Her praise forever:
Both	Holy is Her name!

———— ◇ ————

By M. T. Winter, Crossroad Pub. Co., © 1990 Medical Mission Sisters

Narrator	And Mary remained with Elizabeth three months, [until after the birth of her baby] then returned to her own home.

The Celebration

Narrator	On that day when Elizabeth was due, she gave birth to a son and all the women rejoiced in her delivery — neighbors, family, friends. Eight days later, at the ritual of circumcision, they presumed the boy would be named Zechariah which was his father's name, but his mother said,
Elizabeth	"No! Name him John."
Narrator	Those in charge of the ritual said:
Voice	"None of your relatives bear this name!"
Narrator	They made signs to Zechariah: how would the father have him named? They gave him a writing-tablet, and he wrote: "His name is John." Everyone was astonished. All at once, Zechariah opened his mouth and he spoke, blessing God. Fear filled the neighborhood, and throughout the hill country of Judea people spoke with awe about all that they had seen. Those who heard reflected, saying:
Voice	"What will this child grow up to be? For the hand of God is with him."
Narrator	Filled with the Holy Spirit, Zechariah and Elizabeth sang this prophecy:

———— ◇ ————

◇ **A PSALM OF BENEDICTION** ◇

Elizabeth   Blessed be Shaddai forever!
She has visited Her people.
She liberates us
and through us liberates
all of Her sons and daughters.

Zechariah   We are saved from all who would harm us,
as promised by the prophets
and a covenant of mercy,
so that we might serve Her
fearlessly
in holiness
and in justice
every day,
all the days of our life.

Elizabeth   You, little child, are the prophet
called to prepare Her ways.
Go before Her.
Reveal Her wisdom.
Extend Her tender mercies
with the dawn of this new day,
so that all who sit in the shade of oppression
may walk in the light of the One Who guides
our feet on the paths
of peace.

———— ◇ ————

Narrator   And the child grew strong
            in the Spirit,
            and sojourned in the wilderness
            until the appointed day.

◇ **Points for Shared Reflection**

- Elizabeth's story is so familiar, it is hard to hear it in a different way. Perhaps some new insights have emerged for you after revisiting her story here. If so, share these with each other.

- How do you feel about Elizabeth hearing the news of her conception second hand? Or did she? Did the angel also appear to her? What in the text or your own intuition indicates that this might be so?

- How do you feel about two males, one of whom claims to represent God, making decisions about a woman and her body?

- Scripture says that Mary remained with Elizabeth through the ninth month of her cousin's pregnancy, then left before the birth of John. Do you feel this is an accurate recording of the facts?

- Reflect on the lives and roles of both Elizabeth and Mary — their age, their commissioning, the timing of their pregnancies — and try to discern what God may be saying to the women of today.

◇ **Prayer**

Blessed are You,
O Maker of Miracles,
for giving women
of every age
so many reasons to hope.
May the dawn of a new world order
be born of those among us
who are too old
too young
too poor
and female.
May we be with You,
spinning the future,
boldly believing in You.
Weaver of Dreams,
as we dream the peace,
please make our dream come true.
Women of hope, say Amen!
Women of hope, say: Amen!

———— ◇ ————

MARY

◇ **Scripture Reference**   Luke 1:26–56; 2:1–52; 8:19–21
Matthew 1:18–25; 2:1–23; 12:46–50; 13:53–58
Mark 3:31–35; 6:1–6
John 2:1–12; 19:25–27
Acts 1:14

◇ **Biography**

Scripture states that Mary, mother of Jesus and wife of Joseph, conceived her child miraculously through the intervention of the Holy Spirit while she was still a virgin. After a period of exile to escape Herod's wrath, she made her home in Nazareth. Scripture mentions other children. Her story is told through specific events that focus primarily on her first-born.

◇ **Context**

Our understanding of Mary has been shaped more by proclamation and piety than by historical narrative. In the Roman Catholic tradition, Madonna, Mediatrix, Queen of Heaven and Earth are images honed by religious fervor and to some extent dogma and doctrine. Pious imagination and ecclesiastical regulation have distanced Mary from many women and from women's experience. However, we can have no better model for the present, no better advocate for women's liberation than the one who gave rise within her to the body and blood of the Christ. As we enter into her story here, let us put aside past images and perhaps present prejudice. Here Mary is simply our sister, a woman like any other woman, except for her singular mission. She lived, she died, yet unlike other women, she holds a privileged place in the memory of tradition. The biblical texts that relate to her directly are woven into one narrative here for the lectionary reading, which is set in an interpretive context reflecting the dynamics of feminism today. Mary's story may be celebrated in segments or as a whole, whatever helps us to get in touch with Mary's womanspirit and her female life experience and become engaged with her struggle. As you enter into herstory, look for issues that are similar to your own.

MARY'S STORY

Voice   All who have ears to hear, listen!
This is Mary's story.
This is one woman's story.
This is every woman's story.
Listen, all you who have ears!

I /

**The
ANNOUNCEMENT
Women's Ordination**

◇ **Lectionary Reading**

   Narrator   Six months after Elizabeth conceived,
the angel Gabriel was sent by God
to the Galilean town of Nazareth,
to a virgin betrothed to a man named Joseph,
and the virgin's name was Mary.
The angel said to Mary:

   Angel   "Shalom, O highly favored one;
God Shaddai is with you!"

   Narrator   She was deeply disturbed by these words
and wondered what they might mean.
The angel said to her,

   Angel   "Mary, do not be afraid,
for God is pleased with you.
Listen closely,
you will conceive and bear a child,
and you shall name him Jesus.
He will flourish
and he will be called
the Child of God Most High.
And Shaddai will give to Jesus
the authority of leadership,
to preside over the household of God
and all God's people forever."

   Narrator   Then Mary said to the angel:

   Mary   "How will this happen,
for I am a virgin."

   Angel   "The Holy Spirit will come to you,
the shadow of Shaddai will cover you;
the child you bear will be holy
and will be called the Child of God.
Furthermore, your kinswoman Elizabeth
in her old age
has also conceived a son,
and she who was said to be barren
is already six months pregnant,
for nothing is impossible for God."

   Narrator   And Mary quietly responded,

| Mary | "I am one with the will of God,
let it happen as you say." |

◇ **Response: A Priestly Psalm for Women** (see p. 28)

II /

COMING TOGETHER
Women Celebrate the New Creation

◇ **Lectionary Reading**

Narrator	Soon after, Mary left her village and hurried through the hills of Judea to Elizabeth and Zechariah's home. When Elizabeth heard Mary's greeting, her baby leaped in her womb. Filled with the Holy Spirit, she cried:
Elizabeth	"Blessed are you among women, and blessed is the child in your womb! How can this be, that the mother of my God has come to visit me! The moment your greeting reached my ears, my baby leaped for joy. Blessed are you who dared to believe God's promises to you."
Narrator	Then Mary sang a song of praise.

———— ◇ ————

Mary	My soul celebrates Shaddai!
All	My spirit sings to Shekinah-Shaddai,
Mary	for She erases my anonymity
All	so that all generations of women are blessed.
Mary	She Who has power to open the womb has done great things for me.
All	Holy is Her name.
Mary	Her mercy flows through mother to daughter
All	from generation to generation.
Mary	Her maternal strength strikes at the roots of evil, and it departs.
All	She pushes the proud from the pinnacles of power and lifts up little people.
Mary	She feeds her hungry daughters,
All	but those who are filled to the brim with opportunity, She sends away.
Mary	She soothes all those who turn to Her, remembering Her compassion,
All	keeping Her promise to Sarah and her progeny forever.

—————— ◊ ——————

By M. T. Winter, Crossroad Pub. Co., © 1990 Medical Mission Sisters   *WomanWord* / 15

| Narrator | And Mary remained with Elizabeth three months, [until after the birth of her baby] then returned to her own home. |

◇ **Response: A Psalm for Women-Church** (see p. 30)

III /

**The
BIRTH
Women's Liberation**

◇ **Lectionary Reading**

| Narrator | During the reign of Caesar Augustus, when Quirinius was governor of Syria, a decree was issued requiring a census of all the population. Everyone had to be enrolled, each in their own city. Now Joseph left Nazareth in Galilee for Bethlehem in Judea to register in David's city, for that was his lineage. Mary, his betrothed, who was with child, went to enroll with him. While they were there, the time came for her to deliver. She gave birth to her first-born son, wrapped him in swaddling clothes, and laid him in a manger, because there was no room in the inn. And local shepherds in the fields that night had a vision of an angel radiant in glory, and they were filled with fear. The angel said to them: |
| Angel | "Don't be afraid, I bring good news of incredible joy for you and all the people. Born for you in this city |

	this day
	is a Savior who is the Christ.
	You will find the baby
	swaddled in cloth
	and lying in a manger."
Narrator	And suddenly a multitude of angels appeared
	praising God in song:
Voices	"Glory, glory to El Shaddai
	and peace to all Her people."
All	"Glory, glory to El Shaddai
	and peace to all Her people."
Narrator	When the angels departed,
	the shepherds said:
Shepherds	"Let us go to Bethlehem
	and see for ourselves
	what God has revealed to us."
Narrator	They went with haste
	and found Mary and Joseph
	with the baby,
	who was lying in a manger.
	And they told of the angels
	and all they had heard.
	But Mary reflected
	on all these things
	silently
	in her heart.
	And the shepherds left
	glorifying God
	for all they had heard and seen.

◇ **Response: A Psalm of Bringing to Birth** (see p. 31)

IV /

DEDICATION
Woman Prophet, Woman Pain

◇ **Lectionary Reading**

Narrator	After eight days
	the child was circumcised
	and given the name Jesus,
	the name proclaimed
	by the angel

before he was in the womb.
When the time arrived
for their purification
according to the law of Moses,
his parents took him to Jerusalem
to present him to God,
for according to the law,
every male that opens the womb
is holy before God.
They went to offer sacrifice
according to that law,
a pair of turtledoves
or pigeons.
Now drawn to the temple in Jerusalem
was a devout, dedicated man named Simeon,
whom God had revealed
would not see death
before he had seen the Christ.
Inspired by the Holy Spirit,
he took the child from Mary
and he blessed God
and proclaimed:

───── ◇ ─────

◇ A LEAVE-TAKING PSALM ◇

All   O Holy One of Blessing,
I am ready to go
in peace
now,
touched by Your living word,
for my own eyes
have seen
this day
the good news of salvation,
prepared for all God's people,
made present
in our midst,
a light to reveal You
to unbelievers
and a blessing to all
who believe.

───── ◇ ─────

Narrator   His father and mother marveled
at what was said
about the child.
Simeon blessed them,
and turning to Mary his mother,
he said:

Voice   "This child is destined
for the rise and fall of many
throughout this land;
hidden thoughts
will be revealed,
and pain will pierce you
through and through
like a sword
stabbing your soul."

Narrator   Now Anna,
a widow and prophet,
an elderly, dedicated woman,
approached them,
giving thanks to God,
then went off to proclaim
to all who would listen
the news of the reign of God.
When they had fulfilled all
religious requirements,
Mary and Joseph
returned to Galilee,
to their home in Nazareth.
Now all this had happened
to fulfill God's word
spoken through the prophet:

Voice   "Behold, a virgin will conceive
and she will bear a son,
and his name will be Emmanuel."

Narrator   The name means, God with us.
Now Joseph had not slept with Mary
until she had borne a son,
whom they had named Jesus.

◇ **Response: A Psalm of Dedication** (see p. 32)

V /

SAGES
Women's Wisdom

◇ **Lectionary Reading**

Narrator   Now wise men from the East
came to Jerusalem to inquire:

Sage   "Where is the newborn king of the Jews?
We have seen his star in the East
and we have come to worship him."

Narrator   When Herod the king
heard about this,
he was deeply troubled,
as were many in Jerusalem.
He called together the chief priests and scribes
and asked them,
where was the Christ to be born?
And they answered:

Voice   "In Bethlehem of Judea.
So the prophet has spoken:
'You, Bethlehem,
in the land of Judah,
are no means least among the leaders of Judah;
out of you will come a leader
who will govern Israel.'"

Narrator   Then Herod secretly summoned the sages,
seeking to know when the star had appeared.
And he sent them off to Bethlehem, saying:

Voice   "Search for the child,
and when you have found him,
come back and tell me where he is
so I too may worship him."

Narrator   They left the king
and went their way,
following the star they had seen
in the East.
They were filled with joy
when the star stopped above the place
where the child was living.
They entered Mary's house
and they saw the child with his mother,
and they bowed down
and worshiped him.
They opened their treasures

20 / *WomanWord: MARY*

	and offered to him
	gifts of gold
	and frankincense
	and myrrh.
	Then, warned in a dream
	to avoid Herod,
	they returned to their home
	a different way.
	An angel of God
	then spoke to Joseph
	also in a dream:
Angel	"Get up,
	take the child and his mother
	and run.
	Go down into Egypt
	and remain there,
	until I tell you what to do.
	For Herod is searching for your child,
	and he intends to kill him."
Narrator	He got up, took the child and his mother,
	and fled down to Egypt
	under cover of night,
	where they stayed until Herod had died,
	thereby fulfilling the prophetic word:
Voice	"Out of Egypt have I called my son."
Narrator	Herod, meanwhile,
	when he learned he had been tricked,
	fell into a rage
	and decreed the slaughter
	of every male child in and around Bethlehem
	who was two years old or under,
	fulfilling the prophecy of Jeremiah:
Voice	"A voice was heard in Ramah, wailing:
	Rachel weeping for her children,
	refusing to be comforted
	because they are no more."
Narrator	When Herod died,
	an angel appeared to Joseph
	in a dream, saying:
Angel	"Arise, take the child and his mother,
	and return to the land of Israel,
	for those who would kill him are dead."
Narrator	So Joseph left
	with the child and his mother,

intending to take them home.
But when he learned that Archelaus
was governing Judea,
replacing Herod his father,
he was afraid to go there.
When an angel warned him in a dream,
he emigrated to Galilee
and settled in the city of Nazareth,
thereby fulfilling the prophetic word:

Voice   "He shall be called a Nazarene."

Narrator   And the child grew
and became strong,
and he was full of wisdom,
for he was special to God.

◇ **Response: A Wisdom Psalm** (see p. 33)

VI /

LOSING GOD
Testimony and Tradition

◇ **Lectionary Reading**

Narrator   Every year at Passover
Mary and Joseph went to Jerusalem,
according to ritual custom.
Once when Jesus was twelve years old,
they left for Galilee after the feast,
but the boy remained behind.
His parents were unaware of this,
for the pilgrimage group was large.
After traveling a full day's journey,
they looked among all their family,
inquired of all their acquaintances,
but still they could not find him.
So they returned to Jerusalem seeking him,
and they searched for three full days.
They found him in the temple,
sitting among the rabbis,
listening to them,
questioning them,
amazing them with his intelligence
and his insight
and his answers.

	His anxious parents
	were overcome with relief,
	and his mother said to him,
Mary	"Child, why have you done this to us?
	Your father and I looked everywhere for you,
	and we were growing desperate."
Narrator	Then Jesus said:
Jesus	"Why were you looking for me?
	You should have known
	I would be in God's house."
Narrator	But they did not understand him.
	He went home with them to Nazareth
	and grew up an obedient child.
	But Mary reflected on all these things
	in the quietness of her heart.
	And Jesus increased in wisdom, stature,
	and favor
	with God and with people.

◇ **Response: A Psalm for the Lost and Found** (see p. 34)

VII /

TRANSFORMATION
Transition Time

◇ **Lectionary Reading**

Narrator	There was a wedding in Cana,
	a village in Galilee,
	and Jesus
	and his mother
	were invited to the feast.
	His disciples were also there.
	When they ran out of wine,
	Mary turned to Jesus and said:
Mary	"Child, they have no wine."
Narrator	Jesus replied to his mother:
Jesus	"What am I supposed to do?
	My moment has not yet arrived."
Narrator	But his mother instructed the servants:
Mary	"Do whatever he tells you."

Narrator	Now six stone water jars were there for the customary ritual washing. Each held twenty or thirty gallons. Jesus said to the servants,
Jesus	"Fill the jars with water."
Narrator	And they filled them to the brim. Then Jesus said:
Jesus	"Now draw some out and take it to the steward of the feast."
Narrator	So they drew a sample. And when the chief steward tasted the water that now was wine, he did not know where it had come from, although the servants knew. So the steward called to the bridegroom, saying:
Voice	"Everyone serves the best wine first, so that after the guests have had plenty to drink, they can serve inferior wine. But you have kept the best until last."
Narrator	This was the first of many signs and wonders that Jesus accomplished. It happened at Cana in Galilee, and his disciples believed in him. After that he went down to Capernaum with his mother and brothers and sisters, accompanied by his disciples.

◇ **Response: A Psalm in a Time of Transition** (see p. 35)

VIII /

DISCIPLESHIP
Mothers and Sisters

◇ **Lectionary Reading**

Narrator	Jesus returned to Nazareth, his hometown, and taught in the synagogue on the sabbath. Those who heard him were astonished.
Voice	"Where did this man get his wisdom? Isn't he the carpenter's son?

	Isn't his mother the woman named Mary?

Isn't his mother the woman named Mary?
Aren't James and Joseph and Simon and Jude
his brothers?
Aren't all his sisters living here with us?
Then where did he get all this?"

Narrator They simply could not accept him.
And Jesus said to them:

Jesus "Prophets are only rejected
in their own neighborhood
and in their own house."

Narrator And he did not work many miracles there,
because they did not believe.
One day, while he was teaching,
his mother and his brothers and sisters arrived,
and they waited for him outside.
A messenger told him,

Voice "Your mother and brothers and sisters are here,
and they are asking for you."

Narrator Jesus said:

Jesus "Who are my mother
and my brothers
and my sisters?"

Narrator And looking at those all around him,
he said:

Jesus "Here are my mother
and my brothers
and my sisters!
Whoever does the will of God
is my brother
and my mother
and my sister."

◇ **Response: A Psalm of Relationship with God** (see p. 36)

IX /

CRUCIFIXION
Standing in the Void

◇ **Lectionary Reading**

Narrator Standing by the cross of Jesus
were Mary his mother,
her sister,
Mary the wife of Clopas,
and Mary Magdalene.
When Jesus saw his mother beside
the disciple whom he loved,
he said this to his mother:

Jesus *"Imma'*, there is your son."

Narrator And he said to the disciple,

Jesus "My mother is your mother."

Narrator When Jesus died
the disciple took Mary
into his own home.

◇ **Response: A Psalm of Crucifixion** (see p. 37)

X /

PENTECOST
Female Spirit

◇ **Lectionary Reading**

Narrator They returned to Jerusalem
from the Mount of Olives,
a sabbath day's walk from the city,
and entered the upper room
where they were staying,
Peter and John and James and Andrew,
Philip and Thomas,
Bartholomew and Matthew,
James, the son of Alphaeus,
Simon the Zealot,
and Jude, the son of James.
With one heart they devoted themselves to prayer,
together with the women,
and Mary the mother of Jesus,
and his brothers
and his sisters.

◇ **Response: A Psalm of Spirit** (see p. 38)

◇ **Points for Shared Reflection**

- If you have read Mary's story in its entirety, you may simply want to sit and reflect in silence on all that you have heard, and then share what you are feeling.

- Reflect on the images of Mary that arise from this setting of her story. Compare these with traditional images. Share your own favorite image of her. Does this present image differ from what you preferred in the past? If so, why?

- Consider each scripture passage in terms of the section heading and make connections between your life as a woman today and the life of Mary.

- Consider each scripture passage in light of its accompanying psalm. The scripture transmits the facts as we know them. The psalms are interpretation, both theological and spiritual. How much of what we know of Mary is in the realm of interpretation? What is your response to this interpretation? Add your own perspectives.

◇ **Prayer**

Woman was born of You, Mother God,
yet Jesus was born of a woman
whom we call,
mother of God.
Mother God of the mother of God,
we praise You
as we struggle to comprehend
Your incomprehensible ways.
May we who are sister of Mary
take part in her God-bearing,
God-sharing spirit
for Your greater glory and praise,
now and forever.
Amen.

———— ◇ ————

◇ A PRIESTLY PSALM FOR WOMEN ◇

Leader   Shalom, daughters of God!
Shaddai is pleased with you.

All   How good it is to be called to serve
in the household of Shaddai.

Leader   Thus says Shaddai:
give flesh to the Word of life,
break the bread of justice,
feed all who hunger to take their place
at the table of tradition,
lift the cup of freedom
filled with the saving blood of Christa
who lived and died for us.

All   How can this be for we are female?
The hallowed rites and rituals
exclude women's ways.

Leader   The Child of Shaddai
was born of woman,
God Shaddai first chose a woman
to lead the opening liturgy
of Her own Incarnate Word.
Now every woman
ever after
shares in the primal priesthood
of the woman of Galilee.

All   Praise Shaddai for Her wisdom!
All priesthood is subsidiary,
secondary,
derived,
that does not sink sacramental roots
in Her intuitive grace.

Leader   Thus says Jesus
Who is body and blood of woman
and flesh of her human flesh:
God has anointed me
to preach good news to those deprived,
to release all flesh from bondage,
to liberate from oppression
all who are ritually denied.

All   Praise to You, Anointed One!
When is the appointed time?

Leader   Thus says the Holy Spirit
who transformed Mary of Galilee

into a vessel of the Living God:
Now is the day of deliverance.
Now is the appointed time.
You are the good news God proclaims.
Through you will come the liberating force
to make old structures new.
Women, claim your freedom.
Live your sacred calling.
You are God's anointed.
You are daughters of Shaddai.

All   We praise You, Empowering Spirit,
for the dawning of this promised day.
We are Your waiting celebrants.
Let it happen as You say.

By M. T. Winter, Crossroad Pub. Co., © 1990 Medical Mission Sisters

◇ A PSALM FOR WOMEN-CHURCH ◇

Choir 1   Grace and peace be with you,
            sisters of Elizabeth and Mary.

Choir 2   Blessing and power of Spirit-church
            be with all women of God.

Choir 1   How good and wholesome and holy it is
            for women to come together.

Choir 2   We share our sacred stories,

Choir 1   sift through our graced experience
            and discover common ground,

Choir 2   create our creeds of courage
            and our paradigms of praise.

Choir 1   We hear one another into being,

Choir 2   laugh into life our sterile dreams,
            support the choice taking shape within us.

Choir 1   Women together share new life
            and celebrate miracles:

Choir 2   share how the barren bring to birth,

Choir 1   share the first fruits of believing,

Choir 2   share all the many and marvelous ways
            the Spirit impregnates women
            with the seeds of the new creation
            and the potential for significant change.

Choir 1   Old and young together,

Choir 2   ordinary women together
            break ground for a new world order
            that includes the fringe of society,

Choir 1   is rooted and grounded in justice

Choir 2   and grows strong in the embrace
            of peace.

All   Our soul sings in the strength of Shaddai,
            our spirit rejoices in Her creation!

   By M. T. Winter, Crossroad Pub. Co., © 1990 Medical Mission Sisters

◇ A PSALM OF BRINGING TO BIRTH ◇

Leader　Women, what will we bring to birth
in the world of the new creation?

All　Wisdom and justice,
peace and compassion,
concern for all God's little ones,
for the homeless and the destitute,
the hungry, and all who bear the brunt
of indifference and oppression.

Leader　Women, what will we bring to birth
on the earth of the new creation?

All　A deep respect for our planet,
its windsong and its waters,
its topsoil and its forests,
and a oneness with the wilderness
that is image of our soul.

Leader　Women, what will we bring to birth
in the church of the new creation?

All　A total disdain for power
that diminishes or destroys,
divestment of wealth and status,
a sharing of human resources
based on mutuality
and the sudden surprise of grace.

Leader　Women, what will we bring to birth
in the hearts of the new creation?

All　An unbreakable bond in the Spirit
that binds as one all brothers and sisters,
transcending class, color, culture,
religion, race, and gender,
that treats no personal preference,
no physical or spiritual difference
as aberration or handicap.

Leader　One has been born among us
Who heralds such liberation.
Human liberation,
women's liberation
have taken flesh among us
and in Spirit dwell with us.

All　Holy the woman who helped this happen.
Blessed are we when we give birth
to the Word made flesh
in us.

By M. T. Winter, Crossroad Pub. Co., © 1990 Medical Mission Sisters　　*WomanWord* / **31**

Choir 1   Happy indeed is a dedicated woman;
she is bound to her God securely.

Choir 2   She stands firm and is fed
from the foundations
of her faith.

Choir 1   She walks with wisdom,
accompanied by the revelations
of the ages.

Choir 2   She presents herself
and all she cherishes
humbly before her God.

Choir 1   She speaks her prophetic word
courageously
in the temples of tradition.

Choir 2   She does not fear recrimination,
nor does she flinch from pain.

Choir 1   She offers the fruit of her womb
for a hurting world
and its redemption,

Choir 2   knowing that God accepts the gift
which the world has put aside.

Choir 1   The pain of woman, the sword that slays,
is the cost of her dedication.

Choir 2   A religion demanding her purification
while it holds that males are holy:
this is the sword that slays.

All   Now that our eyes have seen
the salvation of our gender,
we return to those holy places
made believable by grace.

   By M. T. Winter, Crossroad Pub. Co., © 1990 Medical Mission Sisters

◇ A WISDOM PSALM ◇

Leader What good is the gold
that gilds the affluent
and undergirds a two-tier system
in religion
and in the world?

All Follow the One who is simple
and poor
and politically unencumbered.

Leader What good is the incense
that burns with a flair
on the altars of our own making?

All Follow the One
Who worships Shaddai
in spirit and in truth.

Leader What good is the myrrh
that masks the pain
and embalms our dead intentions?

All Follow the One who died
and rose
from the symbols of decay.

Leader You will be offered sage advice
about overpowering others.

All Rather be overpowered
by that power
pressed to a cross.

Leader The way that leads to the center
of success
is strewn with the slaughter
of innocence.

All The way home goes by a different path.
Just follow the song
of the Star.

Leader Wise are the ones who hear this word
and do their best to keep it.

All Wise are the daughters of wisdom,
for they hold these things
in their heart.

By M. T. Winter, Crossroad Pub. Co., © 1990 Medical Mission Sisters

Chorus   Women, we have lost our God.
Tell us where to find Her.

All   Look among your relatives,
inquire of your acquaintances,
search the path of your pilgrimage,
and ask: where is our God?

Chorus   Women, we have lost our God.
Tell us where to find Her.

All   Retrace the routes of religion
and the known roads of your heritage.
Say again the old prayers,
and ask: where is our God?

Chorus   Women, we have lost our God.
Tell us where to find Her.

All   In the temples of tradition,
in the midst of its interpreters,
challenging their assumptions,
questioning presuppositions,
revealing through personal testimony
that in life's experience
God is found,
for She sojourns with Her people.

Chorus   Women, when you find our God,
tell us, so we might worship.

All   We have found Her.
She is with us.
She is dwelling in our heart.

   By M. T. Winter, Crossroad Pub. Co., © 1990 Medical Mission Sisters

◇ A PSALM IN A TIME OF TRANSITION ◇

Choir 1   Our time is in Your hands, O God,
the time of our liberation.

Choir 2   We are filled to the brim with pain
as we await Your transforming Word.

Choir 1   Let the wine flow freely
at the festival of our spirits.

Choir 2   Tell us that woman's plea on behalf of women
has been heard.

Choir 1   Your time is in our hands, O God,
we beg You, delay no longer.

Choir 2   Let the future overlap
our breaking with the past.

Choir 1   Let our time be Yours
for making miracles among us.

Choir 2   And may it really be,
You save the best wine
until last.

By M. T. Winter, Crossroad Pub. Co., © 1990 Medical Mission Sisters

Voice   Who is my mother, my sister?

All   Whoever does the will of God
is mother, daughter, sister.

Voice   Who is my mother, my sister?

All   Whoever does the work of God
is mother, daughter, sister.

Voice   Who is my mother, my sister?

All   Whoever keeps the word of God
is mother, daughter, sister.

Voice   Who is my neighbor?
Who is for me
my mother and my sister?

All   Whoever does the work of justice,
sits beside the wounded
or ministers with compassion,
is our mother and our sister.

Voice   Who is God for me?
Is God really
my mother, my sister?

All   She Who knew you in the womb,
Who gave Her life to shield you
is Shaddai,
is Christa,
loving Mother,
risen Sister.

     By M. T. Winter, Crossroad Pub. Co., © 1990 Medical Mission Sisters

◇ A PSALM OF CRUCIFIXION ◇

Choir 1   Every time a mother loses a child
to drugs, or war,
or the hundred-and-one ways
children die
in the ghettoes of our systems,
Christ dies,
Christa cries.
Shaddai, have mercy on us.

Choir 2   Every time a child gives a mother away,
unable to cope
with the debilitating expense
or condition
of age or illness,
Christ dies,
Christa cries.
Shaddai, have mercy on us.

All   We stand in the midst of our crucifixions,
hugging the deep hole in our center,
feeling the void,
tasting the clotted blood
of suffering,
slow to reach out and ask
for help
as Christ dies,
Christa cries.
Shaddai, have mercy on us.

By M. T. Winter, Crossroad Pub. Co., © 1990 Medical Mission Sisters

◇ A PSALM OF SPIRIT ◇

Choir 1   Come, Holy Spirit,
rattle the rooms
in which we are hiding,
shake the tired foundations
until the institution crumbles,
break the rules
that keep You out of all our
sacred spaces,
then lift from the dust and rubble
a completely new creation.

Choir 2   Come, Holy Spirit,
enter our lives,
whisper our names
and scatter Your gifts of grace
with wild abandon,
give Your silent strength to all imprisoned
by the structures,
and let Your raging fire be our sign
of liberty.

All   Come, Holy Spirit,
help us find ourselves
in vital places,
bringing Your word of freedom
to the poor and the oppressed.
We will remember
women were there
when You burst upon a waiting world
creating and recreating
opportunities
for everyone
to feel and fear
Your face.

 By M. T. Winter, Crossroad Pub. Co., © 1990 Medical Mission Sisters

◇ II ◇
Women and Jesus
in the Spirit
of Shaddai

ANNA

◇ **Scripture Reference**   Luke 2:36–38

◇ **Biography**

Anna, whose husband died after seven years of marriage, remained a widow throughout her long life. Her latter days were spent in prayer and fasting in the Temple enclosure.

◇ **Context**

Anna encountered the infant Jesus when he was brought to the Temple with his parents for his redemption as first-born son.

◇ **Lectionary Reading**

Anna,
Phanuel's daughter,
of the tribe and traditions
of Asher,
a devout,
dedicated woman,
a prophet
able to see
and interpret
the silent, veiled
revelation

of God's mysterious ways,
was seven years a wife
and the rest of her life
a widow.
She remained now
in the Temple,
serving her God
day and night
through ritual fasts
and prayer.
She was eighty-four years young
when she saw the Child
with his mother.
Praising God
for this blessing,
she spoke of the Child
to all concerned
about Israel's liberation,
and from that day,
she preached the miracle
made flesh,
Whom her own eyes had seen.

◇ **Personal Reflection**

Today
the answer came
to me,
setting my soul
at liberty:
it is not a question
of where
as such
or what
or how
or even
how much,
but simply
ensuring time
to be
in touch
with the mystical
side
of me
for days
on end
periodically.

- The wisdom of older wives and widows shines through the pages of scripture. Reflect aloud on the wisdom of Anna. Recall the wisdom of your mother or grandmother or another female elder whom you know.

- Scripture suggests that the God of our biblical tradition favors older women as channels for revealing the depth and extent of God Shaddai's womb-love for us all. Name one or more gifts or blessings from which you or society in general have benefited through the agency of an older woman or "crone."

◇ **Anna's Psalm** (see p. 43)

◇ **Prayer**

God of wisdom,
God of all women,
maidens and mothers,
widows and wives,
look with favor
now, today,
on the greying of our gender.
Aging women carry the cross
of dual discrimination.
May all who are insecure
and anxious
feel themselves set free.
As we grow in age,
may we also grow
in wisdom and grace
and the gracious art
of learning to let go.
May we not be afraid
to speak Your Word
as we await our liberation.
so that on That Day
we may hear You say:
Well done,
you who were faithful,
well done,
and welcome home.
In Christ we say:
Amen.

◇

◇ ANNA'S PSALM ◇

Leader   Sarah, Hannah, Elizabeth, Anna:
Shaddai loves older women.

All   We give thanks and praise to God.

Anna   This is the day which God has revealed.
I am filled to the brim with joy.
Into old age with its limitations,
my God has remembered me.

All   Sarah, Hannah, Elizabeth, Anna:
Shaddai loves older women.
We give thanks and praise to God.

Anna   How long, O God, have I waited
for a sure sign of liberation,
waited with hope,
waited in faith
for the dawning of this day.
And now my heart has feasted upon the One
Who is my salvation.
I have looked into a human face
and have seen the face of God.

All   Sarah, Hannah, Elizabeth, Anna:
Shaddai loves older women.
We give thanks and praise to God.

Anna   No longer will I
or any woman
be the step-child of religion.
No longer will I
or any woman
be barred from the holy places,
or keep God's word,
burning like fire,
locked up inside our heart.
For the One Who has come
is the Word we preach
to every generation,
the Word of truth and Way of life
for all who are oppressed.
Here is the Child of promise.
Here is the Holy of Holies.
Here is the glory of God.

All   Sarah, Hannah, Elizabeth, Anna:
Shaddai loves older women.
We give thanks and praise to God.

By M. T. Winter, Crossroad Pub. Co., © 1990 Medical Mission Sisters

PETER'S MOTHER-IN-LAW

◇ **Scripture Reference** Luke 4:38–39 / Mark 1:29–31
Matthew 8:14–15

◇ **Biography**

We do not know the woman's name nor do we know the name of her daughter. All we know is that she was miraculously cured and was accustomed to her role in the household.

◇ **Context**

Simon Peter invited Jesus into his home where he found his mother-in-law seriously ill and lying in bed with a fever. Jesus cures her and she is immediately concerned with tending to their needs. It is unclear whether Peter is still living there. He may have already left to join Jesus and returned home only to visit.

◇ **Lectionary Reading**

Peter took Jesus home
with him
after they left the synagogue.
He found his mother-in-law
sick in bed,
burning up with fever.
Jesus went to her
and touched her hand,
and all at once
she was cured.
Just as quickly,
she got up
from her bed
and began to wait on them.

◇ **Personal Reflection**

Spirit of God
embrace of God,
brief brush against the face
of God,
bridging the unfathomable space
between this place
in my heart
and God
through life-giving grace,
glory and praise
now
and all days,
alleluia!

◇ **Points for Shared Reflection**

- Three Synoptic Gospels record this incident. What is its significance?
- The narrative about Peter's mother-in-law never mentions Peter's wife. Share your thoughts on this.
- Did the cure symbolize an inner healing of a feverish, red-hot anger toward the man who had left her daughter for a visionary vagabond?
- Do you think the woman was ever reconciled to the fact that a man might leave his wife and family and all his worldly possessions to seek the reign of God?
- What kind of man would leave home so dramatically, then drop in again for a meal?
- What was the plight of a Jewish woman abandoned by her man? From what we know of Jesus and his sense of justice and mercy, how could he possibly have allowed this heart-breaking consequence?

- Did Peter really leave his wife, or was he simply absent from home for extended periods of time?
- Could Peter's wife have been one of the women who accompanied Jesus and his apostles, not simply as wife but as partner in their missionary task?
- Might her mother have encouraged her to join them? Could her mother's cure have convinced her that her husband's behavior was justified? Was the real miracle her conversion to the One Who was responsible for the breakup of her home? How would you respond if this happened to you?
- What meaning is there for women today in this brief biblical narrative?

◇ **A Mother-in-law's Psalm** (see p. 47)

◇ **Prayer**
O God, Shaddai,
You are mother to us
and mother-in-law to many,
to all those whose relationship
is bound by a marriage vow.
May we never forsake or forget You
in our love for one another,
or fail to give thanks
for all the times
You attended to us and our needs.
We, Your children, praise You.
May all of Your children's children
bless Your Holy name,
now and forever.
Amen.

———— ◇ ————

◇ A MOTHER-IN-LAW'S PSALM ◇

All   My God, You are with me always.
My life is in Your hands.

Choir 1   When my child was pulled
from the warmth of my womb,
You were there
to instruct and encourage,
as midwife to my spirit,
as wet nurse for my soul.

Choir 2   When my child was pulled
from my hearth and home
by one who would claim her
completely,
You taught me how to graciously share
that birth bond
with another,
then gave me my children's children
to comfort my empty arms.

Choir 1   I give thanks for Your maternal presence.
My heart overflows with joy,

Choir 2   for my blessings indeed
have multiplied
and my faith in You abides.

Choir 1   Yet who can know Your plan for us
or understand Your ways?

Choir 2   You call us,
and we answer,
no matter what the consequence
or the cost
to the ones we love.

All   Blessed are you Who dares to promise
a happy ever after.

Choir 1   You heal our ills
and calm the fears
and fires that rage
within us.

Choir 2   Help us to faithfully follow You
and to serve You
without compromise
every day of our mortal lives.

All   All that You do is holy,
and holy is Your name.

By M. T. Winter, Crossroad Pub. Co., © 1990 Medical Mission Sisters

WOMAN ACCUSED OF ADULTERY

◇ **Scripture Reference**   John 8:2–11

◇ **Biography**

The only biographical information identifying this woman is the accusation by the scribes and Pharisees that she had committed a sin.

◇ **Context**

A woman caught in the act of adultery is brought to trial by the scribes and Pharisees. They make Jesus the judge and jury. She has already been condemned to death according to the Law of Moses. The penalty for adultery is execution. Married women were usually strangled. Betrothed virgins were always stoned. Witnesses against the accused were supposed to initiate the execution. However, the Law clearly states that both the woman and the man who commit adultery are to be put to death (Lev 20:10; Deut 22:22–23). No mention is made of this fact by those who make the accusation.

◇ **Lectionary Reading**

At daybreak,
Jesus returned to the Temple.
People crowded around him
as he began to teach.
The scribes and Pharisees
dragged a woman
into the presence of Jesus,
and in full view of everyone,
made this accusation.
"Rabbi," they said,
"this woman here
has been caught in the act
of adultery.
The Law commands we condemn her
to death.
The Law says
we should stone her.
Tell us,
what do you say?"
Now this was a test,
for they were seeking something
to use against him.
But Jesus ignored their question,
and with the tip of his finger,
started scribbling
on the ground.
They persisted until
he broke his silence.
Looking up, he said:
"Let the one among you
who has not sinned
be the first to throw a stone."
Then bending down,
he scribbled some more,
as one by one,
those who condemned her
silently slipped away.
Jesus was alone with the woman.
"Where have they gone?"
he asked her.

"Tell me, has no one condemned you?"
"No one, sir," she answered.
"And neither do I," said Jesus.
"Go now and sin no more."

◇ **Personal Reflection**

Love
is a tapestry
we weave
into patterns
we believe
from jumbled skeins
and tangled threads.
Between
the knots
no clear design
emerges
from what I see.
What image
do You perceive
O Love Divine
when You look back
at me?

◇ **Points for Shared Reflection**

- The accused woman was caught in the act of adultery. Why didn't they accuse the man? Compare the attitudes reflected here with attitudes today.

- Commentaries do not tell us that both man and woman are to be put to death, according to the Law of Moses. Discuss this blatantly sexist slant to contemporary interpretation.

- What were the woman's accusers trying to trap Jesus into saying or doing? Were they daring him to accuse them of violating the Law?

- What do you suppose Jesus was scribbling on the ground?

- Of all the times this text has appeared in the lectionary cycle, have you ever heard a sermon about the missing man?

- A central theme here is certainly forgiveness, but more fundamental are the related themes of justice and gender discrimination. In what ways does this woman's story proclaim a word of hope for us all?

◇ **A Psalm of the Accused** (see p. 52)

Forgiving God,
All-Giving God,
in human flesh
the Living God,
accused, abused,
and executed,
You know what it means
to be put on trial,
humiliated,
condemned.
Be with those who are persecuted,
with women who are prosecuted,
with all who are accused,
with all who are condemned,
with all who are victims
of unjust structures,
sexist systems,
lying tongues.
May those who have taken advantage
of our feelings
and our flesh
be confronted by Your justice
and converted by Your grace.
May their victims
find that peace
which surpasses understanding,
and may their wounded souls
and spirits
be healed by Your embrace,
through Christ our Love.
Amen.

―――― ◇ ――――

Choir 1   O God, come to my rescue,
for the weapons of war
surround me
and the violent
ring me round.

Choir 2   Like a fawn in the thicket,
pursued by hounds,
I tremble before
my accusers,
knowing there is no recourse
among those who would bring me down.

Choir 1   I do not insist on my innocence,
for indeed,
I confess
I have sinned.

Choir 2   I seek only justice and mercy,
and from you, my God,
forgiveness,
and a chance to try again.

Choir 1   You, O God, are my refuge,
my haven in times of terror,
my hope during days of despair.

Choir 2   You lift me out of the jaws of death
to a place of security and safety
in the hollow of Your wings.

Choir 1   Now I who have died
am alive,
and grateful.

Choir 2   To You will I sing
a thanksgiving hymn
every day
all the days
of my life.

    By M. T. Winter, Crossroad Pub. Co., © 1990 Medical Mission Sisters

WIDOW OF NAIN

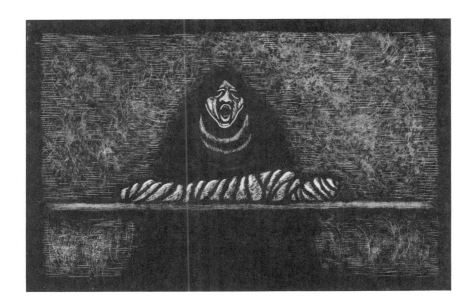

◇ **Scripture Reference**   Luke 7:11–17

◇ **Biography**

The woman is a widow about to bury her only son. She lives in the village of Nain, which is about three walking hours southeast of Nazareth.

◇ **Context**

Jesus and his followers encounter a funeral procession near the gate of the village of Nain. The themes of death and resurrection recall an ancient Elijah story, when the prophet raised up a widow's son and restored him to his mother (1 Kgs 17:17–24).

◇ **Lectionary Reading**

Now Jesus was heading toward the town of Nain
accompanied by his disciples
and many other people.
Near the gate of the town
they encountered
a large funeral procession.
Many of the town's inhabitants
were with a widow
who was on her way
to bury her only son.

When Jesus saw the woman,
he felt sorry for her
and spoke to her,
telling her not to cry.
Touching the bier,
he called aloud,
"Young man,
I bid you rise!"
The dead son rose
and began to speak.
Jesus gave him to his mother.
Fear filled all
who were standing by.
They glorified God,
crying aloud:
"A great prophet
has risen among us;
God has visited our people."
The news of what had happened here
spread throughout Judea
and the surrounding countryside.

◇ **Personal Reflection**

A swirling
whirlwind
whipped
through flimsy defenses
to strip
with centrifugal force
feelings
and fears
leaving no alternative
but to redress
naked essentials
with song.
Mighty One,
why am I
who am I
what am I
will it be long
before everything
winter weakens
wakens to spring?

- A woman mourns her only son. Do you think she had any daughters?

- Why was it particularly tragic in first-century Judaism to lose one's only son?

- Jesus felt sorry for the woman. Jesus may have felt sorry for all women. Why might he feel that way?

- What in this biblical story especially touches you? What message does it proclaim here and now?

◇ **A Widow's Psalm** (see p. 56)

◇ **Prayer**

Blessed are You,
O Tie That Binds
one person to another
in the miracle of love.
O Everlasting Moment,
O Hope That Never Dies,
be with the one
devastated
by death's visitation.
Be her life in death,
her hope in despair,
her promise of love everlasting,
now and forever.
Amen.

———— ◇ ————

All   All you who keep at a distance,
come near and see my sorrow,
come close and feel my pain.
The love of my life has been taken away.
I shall never be whole again.

Choir 1   As I stand alone in the shadow of death,
I see no green in my valley,
no flower beside my path;
no birdsong breaks the silent void
around my broken heart.

Choir 2   The light has been extinguished.
How can I carry on?
It is hard to hold onto the vision,
hard to find any meaning,
hard to keep on going
when the point of it all is gone.

Choir 1   O God of the Resurrection,
allow me to take my comfort
in the flesh our flesh created.
Let our spirit live on forever
in the offspring of our love.

Choir 2   May the child of my girlhood passion
lift me again into laughter
and be there with me
when the trumpet sounds
for me
from my heavenly home.

All   May the one I mourn
be waiting for me
and remain with me forever.
Hear me, heed me, Shaddai!

    By M. T. Winter, Crossroad Pub. Co., © 1990 Medical Mission Sisters

WOMAN WITH THE FLOW OF BLOOD

◊ **Scripture Reference**   Mark 5:25–34 / Luke 8:43–48
Matthew 9:20–22

◊ **Biography**

All three accounts record that this woman has suffered an incurable flow of blood for twelve years. For all that time she has been ritually unclean, as indicated in the Law. "If a woman has a flow of blood outside her period, or if her period is prolonged, as long as the flow lasts she shall be unclean, the same as for her monthly periods" (Lev 15:25). The woman was a Galilean. Nothing more is known of her.

◊ **Context**

This woman's story is inserted into the Synoptic accounts of the raising of Jairus's daughter. The child is as old as the woman's illness, establishing a literary link. Both accounts ordinarily occur together. While there is value in exploring their connections, it is also worthwhile considering each story separately, as they are presented here.

◊ Lectionary Reading

There was a woman
in the crowd around Jesus
who had suffered
from a flow of blood
for twelve years.
Various doctors were unable to cure her.
After long and painful treatment,
she had spent all her money
and was not any better.
In fact, she was getting worse.
"If I but touch his clothes,"
she had told herself,
"I will be well again."
She came up behind Jesus,
reached out,
and touched the tassel
on his garment,
and she was instantly cured.
"Who touched me?"
Jesus shouted.
"The crowd is pressing upon you,"
said Peter.
"What do you mean, 'who touched me?'"
But he searched the crowd, insisting,
"I felt power go out from me.
I want to know who touched me."
Trembling, the woman came forward
and threw herself at his feet.
Jesus said,
"My daughter,
your faith was the source
of your healing.
Be free,
and go in peace."

◊ Personal Reflection

When a young girl
bleeds
in a woman's way,
she refrains
from Eucharist
in Ghana
I am told.
When a woman
bleeds

on days between
the months
she is with child,
she cooks
and eats
her meals
apart
because
she is defiled,
so several wives
for the man
you see
are a practical
necessity,
a tradition
from of old.
Jesus,
the blood
of the woman
who bled
mingles
with the blood
You shed,
as a sign
of contradiction,
for it has been
revealed:
who touches
the hem
of Your justice
absolutely
will be healed,
but not without
crucifixion.
Now what
will it take
to stop the flood
of discrimination
associated
with blood?

- Commentators refer to an issue of blood. Blood was indeed an issue, of life and death, of genealogy, of religious and social segregation and of gender discrimination. Name the justice issues still associated with blood.

- To touch is to tap into power. How can we touch Jesus so that power comes to us?

- To liberate is to empower and to empower is to heal. What is there within you or in society in general that needs a liberating touch?

◇ **A Woman's Psalm** (see p. 61)

◇ **Prayer**

Blessed are You,
Holy One Who Bleeds.
You spill Your sacred juices
over all who call Your name,
setting Your seal
irrevocably
on the female enterprise.
You share Your deepest secret,
the mystery of fecundity,
with those who are bound
by blood to You
in a covenant of love.
May we not take this privilege lightly,
but may we always cherish
the gift so uniquely ours.
Protect us
against all violence
from outside
or within,
and keep us free
to choose our grace
from all You so graciously offer
every day of our life.
Amen.

——— ◇ ———

All   Holy the Blood poured out for me
as a testament of love,
a pledge of faith,
a reconciliation.

Holy the Blood that comes into me
through the cup of a new covenant,
the cup of my salvation.

Holy the blood that flows through me,
the blood of life,
my mother's blood,
my grandmother's blood,
the blood of her mother's mother
and the lineage of generations.

Holy the blood spilling out of me,
cleansing flood,
liberating blood.
A woman's blood is holy.

A bleeding woman images Christ
and all of her
is holy.

A woman bleeds.
Christa bleeds.
Jesus nailed to a crossbeam
bleeds.

Blood is the symbol of death to life.
We thank You and praise You, Shaddai.

By M. T. Winter, Crossroad Pub. Co., © 1990 Medical Mission Sisters

JAIRUS'S DAUGHTER

◇ **Scripture Reference**   Mark 5:21–24, 35–43
Luke 8:40–42, 49–56
Matthew 9:18–19, 23–26

◇ **Biography**

The little girl who was twelve years old was the daughter of a synagogue official. Luke says she was his only daughter. She may have been his only child and she probably lived in Capernaum in Galilee.

◇ **Context**

This story is interrupted by the account of a second miracle story, the healing of the woman with an incurable flow of blood. As told by Mark and Luke, the little girl is still alive when Jairus first approaches Jesus to ask him to save her life. In Matthew's heavily edited summary, the child has already died. These two miracle stories concerning the lives of two women, one mature, the other approaching puberty, are presented as a unit in scripture.

◇ **Lectionary Reading**

After Jesus had crossed the lake by boat,
a large crowd gathered around him,
and they remained by the side of the lake.
A synagogue official named Jairus
made his way through the swarm of people
and fell down at the feet of Jesus, pleading,
"My little daughter is dying.
Come, lay your hands on her;
heal her and save her life."
As he was speaking,
members of his household arrived.
"Your daughter is dead," they told him.
"Do not trouble the Master any more."
Hearing this, Jesus said to the man,
"Have faith. Do not be afraid."
Approaching the official's house,
Jesus heard all the commotion,
the sound of the musicians,
the unrestrained weeping and wailing.
"Why are you crying?" he asked them.
"The child is not dead. She is sleeping."
The mourners laughed at him.
Sending everyone away
except the little girl's mother and father
and Peter and James and John,
he entered the place where the child was lying,
took her by the hand and said,
"Talitha kum! ... Little girl, get up!"
She got up at once and began to walk.
Her parents were astonished.
He told them to give her something to eat.
And the news of what had happened spread
throughout the countryside.

◇ **Personal Reflection**

In a little while
I will not be,
so forgive me
my intensity.

It is
as if somehow
I fear
I will not long
inhabit here.
I feel a force
ten thousand times
the pull of earth
compelling me
toward some deep
destined
reality,
while the child
in me
is struggling to cling
momentarily
to some known
nurturing.

◇ **Points for Shared Reflection**

- What is the message of this story and what is its significance for women?

- A little girl lies buried deep in the heart of every woman. Get in touch with your own little girl and call her to life again.

- Reflect on this story in relationship to the story of the woman with the flow of blood (p. 57). In what ways are they connected? What meanings emerge when both miracle stories are seen in light of each other?

◇ **A Little Girl's Psalm** (see p. 65)

◇ **Prayer**

Good Mother God,
I call to You
from the far side of the morning,
from the wellspring of the past.
Raise up to life within me
the child of Your new creation,
the child of imagination,
to love, laugh, live to the full
the good news of belonging
to the household of Your grace.
Let me live to see You face to face,
in this world and in the world to come,
Good Mother God.
Amen.

——— ◇ ———

◇ A LITTLE GIRL'S PSALM ◇

Choir 1   Dear God, this is Your daughter.
Teach me how to pray.

Choir 2   Dear God, Your world is wonderful.
Come on out and play.

Choir 1   Spill Your sun on my sandals.
Weave me a daisy chain
to tickle my toes when I dip and dance
to the drumbeat of Your rain.

Choir 2   Let's run 'til we drop in Your meadow,
and skip 'til Your sun goes down.
Let's never end our "let's pretend."
I'll clap, You come as a clown.

Choir 1   You tell me so many secrets.
How very wise You are.
Promise me You'll hear me
when I wish upon a star.

Choir 2   May Your green woods last forever.
May I never grow too tall
to imagine You inside of me,
to hear You when You call.

Choir 1   Dear God, You know I love You.
What else is there to say?

Choir 2   Dear God, Your world is wonderful.
Thank You for another day.

By M. T. Winter, Crossroad Pub. Co., © 1990 Medical Mission Sisters   *WomanWord* /

WOMAN WHO ANOINTS JESUS' HEAD

◇ **Scripture Reference**   Mark 14:3–9 / Matthew 26:6–13

◇ **Biography**

Nothing is known of this woman except her beautiful, prophetic gesture, which remains in memory of her.

◇ **Context**

The importance of this anointing has been lost in light of the Lucan and Johannine records of the anointing of Jesus' feet. The fact that there were three different women in these similar accounts has been minimized as well. The action takes place two days before the Passover and is situated in both Gospels in the context of the Passion narrative. Elisabeth Schüssler Fiorenza entitled her groundbreaking feminist theological study *In Memory of Her*, emphasizing the significance of this anointing, a prophetic recognition of Jesus as the Christ, and of this female whom Jesus wanted us all to remember and patriarchy ensured that we would not, until now.

◇ **Lectionary Reading**

Jesus was having dinner
in Bethany
at the house of Simon the leper
when a woman came in
with an alabaster jar
of pure and costly ointment.
She broke the jar
and poured the ointment
over the head of Jesus.
Some who were present
were indignant.
"For what purpose is this waste?
Ointment like this could have been sold
for more than three hundred denarii,
and the money given to the poor."
And they were angry with her.
But Jesus said,
"Let her alone.
Why do you trouble her?
This beautiful thing
she has done for me.
As for the poor,
you can do good to them
whenever you wish.
The poor you will always have with you.
You will not always have me.
She has done what was in her power to do.
She anointed my body for burial.
Truly, I assure you,
wherever throughout the whole world
this Gospel is proclaimed,
what she has done
will be told
in memory of her."

◇ **Personal Reflection**

There is more here
than meets the eye:
out of the depths
a fierce desire
to be one
with the One I feel
as fire.

◇ **Points for Shared Reflection**

- What is the significance of this story and why is it particularly important for women?

- Contrast this account with the one of the woman anointing the feet of Jesus and note the distinctions between them, both in action and in meaning.

- Comment on the promise of Jesus, that wherever in the world this Gospel is proclaimed, it will be told in memory of her. Has the promise really been fulfilled?

- What about the poor? Reflect on what was said on their behalf by the indignant and by Jesus. What is your response?

◇ **An Anointing Psalm** (see p. 69)

◇ **Prayer**

Come, O Holy Spirit,
O Sanctifying Spirit,
fill our hearts,
fill our lives
with the feel of Your fiery Presence,
so that all that we do,
all that we are,
comes from You
within us.
Anoint us now,
so that from this day
we are Your disciples only,
committed to carrying out faithfully
Your mission in the world,
now and always.
Amen.

———— ◇ ————

All   Anoint me with the oil of integrity, O God,
and the seal of Your sanctifying Spirit.

Choir 1   Anoint my head so that all of my thoughts
come forth from the well of Your Being
to fill me with grace and peace.

Choir 2   Anoint my eyes so that I might see
Your Presence and Providence clearly.

Choir 1   Anoint my ears that I might hear
the cry of the poor all around me
and the whisper of Your word.

Choir 2   Anoint my lips that I might proclaim
the Good News of Your mission
and the meaning of Jesus the Christ.

Choir 1   Anoint my hands to hold and heal
the many lives that are broken,
that I may do good,
do what I must
to bring hope into hopelessness.

Choir 2   Anoint my feet to walk in Your ways,
to run and never grow weary,
to stand up for justice unafraid.

Choir 1   Anoint my heart with warmth
and compassion
and a genuine generosity
toward all who are in need.

Choir 2   Anoint the whole of me,
O Holy One,
that I too may be holy.

Choir 1   Anoint my spirit for mission,
that I might reach out
and into
the heart of the whole
hurting world.

Choir 2   Anoint my soul for ministry,
that I might have the courage
to respond with the whole of my being
to the daily demands of grace.

All   Anoint me with the oil of integrity, O God,
and the seal of Your sanctifying Spirit.

By M. T. Winter, Crossroad Pub. Co., © 1990 Medical Mission Sisters

WOMAN WHO ANOINTS JESUS' FEET

◇ **Scripture Reference**   Luke 7:36–50

◇ **Biography**

The woman of this story has long been confused with Mary of Bethany, who also anointed the feet of Jesus (Jn 12:1–8), and at times with Mary Magdalene, from whom, so they say, seven devils had been expelled. It is assumed that the woman who approaches Jesus in the house of Simon the Pharisee is a sinner. We know she is a Galilean. We do not know her name.

Tradition has confused this account with two other incidents: the anointing of the feet of Jesus in the house of his friends in Bethany, and the anointing of his head by a woman when he was a guest of Simon the leper. This story is the one remembered. Much is made of the unchallenged assumption that the woman was a public sinner, but that fact is unsubstantiated. While the passage illustrates the integral connection between loving and the forgiveness of sins and the preceding text calls attention to the fact that Jesus associates with sinners, the woman's sin may be no more than that associated with her status or a pattern of behavior unacceptable to the male ruling class.

◇ **Lectionary Reading**

One of the Pharisees,
Simon by name,
invited Jesus to a meal.
When he arrived at his house
and was seated at table,
a woman who had a bad name
in the town
came into the house
carrying
an alabaster jar of ointment.
She came up behind Jesus,
weeping,
and bent down to anoint his feet.
Her tears fell on the feet of Jesus.
She wiped them away with her hair,
kissed his feet
and anointed them
with the ointment from her jar.
Simon seeing this
said to himself:
"If this man were really a prophet,
he would know what kind of woman this is,
he would know her reputation,
he would know who was touching him."
"Simon," said Jesus,
discerning his thoughts,
"A creditor once
had two men in his debt.
The one owed him five hundred denarii,
the other owed him fifty.
Since neither was able to pay him back,
he pardoned both of them.
Which one loved him more?"

"The one who was pardoned more,
I suppose,"
was Simon's reluctant reply.
Then Jesus turned to the woman.
"Simon, do you see this woman?
I came into your house,
and you, the host,
poured no water over my feet,
but she has covered my feet with tears
and dried them with her hair.
You gave me no kiss,
but she has been covering my feet
with kisses
ever since I arrived.
You did not anoint my head with oil,
but she has anointed my feet with ointment.
You say her sins are many.
Then her many sins must have been forgiven
because she has loved so much,
for the one who is forgiven a little,
loves only a little bit."
Then Jesus turned to the woman and said,
"Go in peace. Your sins are forgiven,
because you love so much."

◇ **Personal Reflection**

Center me
enter me
mystical
Mystery,
cleanse me
and quiet me,
tell me
Thou art
the thin thread
of hope
that sustains
my believing,
the rush
of content
that inhabits
my heart.

◇ **Points for Shared Reflection**

• Why did Luke include this particular story in his Gospel?

• The woman had a bad reputation. What do you suppose that means? Name some of the things she might have done to acquire a bad name in her town.

• What are some of the things feminists do or say today that have given them a bad name in church or in society?

• Whether or not the woman was a "sinner" in the public sense of the term, why do you think she approached Jesus and why did she act as she did?

• New Testament translations and commentaries disagree on which is the more accurate wording, that her sins were forgiven because she loved much, or she loved much because her sins were forgiven. Which do you prefer?

◇ **An Outcast's Psalm** (see p. 74)

◇ **Prayer**

We turn to You and Your mercy,
O God of barren places
and friend of the oppressed.
We stand in need of conversion,
from pain to peace,
from sadness to joy,
from guilt to affirmation.
Lead us not into isolation,
but deliver us from anger,
for Yours is the kindness,
the patience,
the strength we desire,
now and forever.
Amen.

———— ◇ ————

All　My God, my God, have pity on me,
　　　for I am greatly afflicted.

Choir 1　My heart is heavy laden,
　　　my sorrow is like a stone
　　　that weighs me down and paves the road
　　　on which I walk alone.

Choir 2　I live on the margins of meaning,
　　　an outcast, forced to choose,
　　　above all else, survival.
　　　I have nothing left to lose.

Choir 1　I hurry through public places,
　　　hard pressed to outrun my shame,
　　　fearing the pointed gossip
　　　that pierces me with blame.

Choir 2　Those who would call me sinner.
　　　fail to understand
　　　the burden of life I carry,
　　　and never lend a hand.

Choir 1　My nights are filled with weeping,
　　　my days approach despair.
　　　How shall I sing the song I know
　　　is unwelcome everywhere?

Choir 2　I lift my life to Your justice,
　　　I lift my love to Your own,
　　　and wait on Your word,
　　　like a lingering bird
　　　when all of its flock have flown.

Choir 1　Let me touch the feet of Your mercy,
　　　let me wash them with my tears.
　　　Let me hear Your word of comfort
　　　dispelling all my fears.

Choir 2　Then my soul will sing of Your goodness,
　　　and the earth will repeat the song,
　　　'til the sweet-smelling oil of gladness
　　　anoints me and makes me strong.

Choir 1　My God, I am sorely afflicted.
　　　It is more than I can bear.

Choir 2　Deliver me from evil.
　　　Have pity and hear my prayer.

All　My God, my God, have pity on me,
　　　for I am greatly afflicted.

　　　By M. T. Winter, Crossroad Pub. Co., © 1990 Medical Mission Sisters

CRIPPLED WOMAN

◇ **Scripture Reference**   Luke 13:10–17

◇ **Biography**

The woman whom the text refers to as a daughter of Abraham is crippled with a condition that leaves her permanently bent over and unable to stand up straight. She has had this affliction for eighteen years.

◇ **Context**

Jesus encounters the crippled woman in one of the synagogues where he was teaching on the sabbath. The general assumption is that the woman's condition is the result of demonic possession. His decision to heal her on the sabbath, publicly and in a house of prayer, proclaims yet again his message that people take priority over regulations and rules.

◇ **Lectionary Reading**

One sabbath day
Jesus was teaching
in one of the synagogues.
A woman was there
who lived eighteen years
with a crippling condition
that left her bent over double
and unable to stand up straight.

75

Jesus saw her
and called her
to come to him.
Laying his hands upon her,
he said,
"You are rid of your infirmity."
She straightened up
immediately
and gratefully
glorified God.
The synagogue official
was angry with Jesus
because he had healed
on the sabbath,
and he announced to all
who were present:
"There are six days
each week
for manual labor.
Come and be healed
on one of those days.
Do not come on the sabbath."
But Jesus gave this reply.
"How hypocritical!
Do you not untie your donkey
or your ox
and take it for water
on the sabbath?
This woman,
this daughter of Sarah,
has been held in bondage
for eighteen years.
Why not release her
on the sabbath?"
His adversaries were filled
with confusion,
but the people were filled
with joy
at his wonders
and his words.

Personal Reflection

Bent
over
a fist full
of twigs
twice daily,
sweeping.
Bent
beneath
a load
of wood
or care.
Keeping
the rules
keep a woman
bent
by burdens,
spent
with weeping.
A woman
is bent.
Surely
You meant
when You lifted
her up
long ago
to Your praise,
Compassionate One,
not one woman
only,
but all women
bent
by unbending ways.

◇ **Points for Shared Reflection**

- In what ways are women crippled by the burdens they must bear?

- Do you agree with Jesus that people take priority over religious regulations? Has the church of your experience resembled Jesus in this regard?

- Reflect on an inner or an external concern that is presently weighing you down. Pray to Jesus to lift this burden, and if you so choose, share your burden with another person.

◇ **A Psalm for the Heavily Burdened** (see p. 79)

◇ **Prayer**

Holy are You,
O One Who Sings
the song of the new creation,
in Whom there is no separation
into hierarchical clusters
of gender, race, or class.
As we await that redemptive moment
of our cosmic liberation,
let us work to release from bondage
all who are imprisoned
in the quiet desperation
of their little locked lives.
Holy are You,
O One Who Frees.
We need Your affirmation
now and forever.
Amen.

———— ◇ ————

◇ A PSALM FOR THE HEAVILY BURDENED ◇

Choir 1   Look upon me, have mercy on me,
                 O Source of my liberation,
                 for I am heavily burdened.

Choir 2   The cares I carry are weighing me down.
                 I am losing all perspective.
                 My eyes no longer see the stars
                 in this never-ending night.

Choir 1   I am crippled by fear and anxiety
                 when I think of the world
                 we are handing on
                 to succeeding generations:

Choir 2   bombs that may blow us all to bits,
                 polluted streams and rivers,
                 wizards, fads, and charlatans
                 in place of sacred shrines.

Choir 1   I am crippled by institutional rules
                 and insensitive regulations,
                 burdened by expectations,
                 by wishes that won't come true.

Choir 2   I am crippled by gender bondage
                 and the yoke this lays upon me
                 and all women of the world,
                 and I fear the rage
                 that rises in me
                 when my sisters
                 are denied.

Choir 1   Bend down to me and lift me up
                 to face myself with courage,
                 to look the demonic straight in the eye
                 and resist it with a song.

Choir 2   Let me see to another's sorrow,
                 share another's injustice,
                 bear another's burdens,
                 and in the process,
                 lose my own.

All   Teach me to care and not to care,
                 bid my fear,
                 be still,
                 and let all my insecurity
                 lose itself
                 in Your will.

By M. T. Winter, Crossroad Pub. Co., © 1990 Medical Mission Sisters   *WomanWord* / 79

POOR WIDOW

◇ **Scripture Reference**   Mark 12:41–44 / Luke 21:1–4

◇ **Biography**

Scripture tells us only that the woman was poor and that she was a widow. She must have lived in Jerusalem or in a village nearby.

◇ **Context**

Mark and Luke place this story at the end of Jesus' ministry. Because parallel accounts of the story are found in Jewish and other literature, some commentators suspect it may originally have been a parable made into an incident in Jesus' ministry in order to illustrate a point, perhaps about almsgiving.

◇ **Lectionary Reading**

Jesus sat watching people
put money
into the temple treasury.
The rich were usually generous.
Then he saw an impoverished widow
putting in her two small coins.
He called to his disciples and said:
"This poor widow's gift
is worth far more

than all other contributions,
for they gave of their abundance
from the money they had left over,
while she gave all the money she had
from the little she had to live on."

◇ **Personal Reflection**

Holy
the hand
embracing
the plough
the faceless oppressed
the breast
of compassion
nourishing
now.
Holy Holy
the heart that disarms
the faith that inflames
the wisdom
that warms.
Holy Holy Holy
transcendence
incarnate
in clay
creating the best
of all
we have wasted
today.

◇ **Points for Shared Reflection**

- This story is paradigmatic of several contemporary justice issues, notably, the inequity between haves and have-nots, and the feminization of poverty. What does this Gospel story say to realities such as these?

- Consider the irony of a poor woman giving her all to the wealthy, male-dominated religious institution, with inadequate recompense. What parallels come to mind between her experience and your own?

◇ **A Psalm on Behalf of the Poor** (see p. 83)

◇ **Prayer**

God of the poor,
God who was poor,
You entered human history
impoverished and homeless,
and fled in search of refuge
to a land that was not Your own.
You understand the meaning
of the poverty of deprivation,
whether body, mind, or spirit,
temporary or indefinite,
of culture, class, or gender,
anywhere in the world.
Give to the hearts
of all the poor
a wealth of benediction,
both temporal and eternal,
and good things in abundance
for the enrichment of their lives.
We turn to You,
we pray to You,
You who feed the hungry:
give shelter to the homeless
and heal the brokenhearted,
until You come again.
Amen.

——— ◇ ———

◇ A PSALM ON BEHALF OF THE POOR ◇

Choir 1   Helpless are the poor, Shaddai,
             for the poor do not have access
             to the bounty of the earth.

Choir 2   Homeless are the poor, Shaddai;
             they lack the opportunity
             for shelter and security
             in time of dire need.

Choir 1   Hungry are the poor, Shaddai;
             they dream at night of lavish feasts,
             at dawn, of daily bread.

Choir 2   Without hope are the poor, Shaddai,
             when promises all trickle down
             to nothing but despair.

Choir 1   How long must the poor cry out to You
             and wait to receive an answer?

Choir 2   How long can we keep faith in You,
             so silent to our need?

Choir 1   Forgive us our doubts and addictions,
             our escape from desperation.

Choir 2   Give us the strength and fortitude
             to wait upon Your word.

Choir 1   May the morning star bring hope to all
             in the midst of destitution.

Choir 2   May evening find the poor at rest
             in Your everlasting arms.

Choir 1   On That Day the poor will dance
             through all the streets of heaven.

Choir 2   On That Day there will be no trace
             of inequality.

Choir 1   Blessed are You, God of the Poor,
             Mother of all Your children.

Choir 2   We cling to the breasts of Your abundance,
             and gratefully drink our fill.

By M. T. Winter, Crossroad Pub. Co., © 1990 Medical Mission Sisters   *WomanWord* / **83**

CANAANITE WOMAN AND HER DAUGHTER

◇ **Scripture Reference**   Mark 7:24–30 / Matthew 15:21–28

◇ **Biography**

The woman is a Gentile, a Greek, by birth a Syrophoenician, by religion a Canaanite. To the Jews she was a pagan, a foreigner to their culture and outside the covenant. For this she was despised. She is persistent and unrelenting, willing to endure humiliation on behalf of her suffering child. The depth of her faith in Jesus is the basis of her daughter's miraculous release from demonic possession. All we know of the young girl is what we hear from her mother's pleas.

◇ **Context**

After his rejection in Galilee, Jesus enters Tyre and Sidon, Gentile territory in southern Phoenicia, what we call Lebanon. Jesus performs a miracle at a distance in response to a woman's tenacity and faith. Her words, not the words or the miracle of Jesus, are the climax of the story, For this reason, the incident is unique. This story is also about Jews and Gentiles and may have been preserved because it addresses the disputed question of limits. How far does the mission of Jesus extend? Apparently to wherever faith is found. The harsh words on the lips of Jesus may well reflect this struggle within the post-Resurrection church.

Jesus withdrew to the region
of Tyre and Sidon.
He did not want anyone to know
he was there,
but he was soon recognized.
A Canaanite woman
came up to him
and threw herself
at his feet, pleading:
"Have mercy on me
and my daughter,
for she is possessed
by a devil."
Jesus did not say a word.
She persisted
until the disciples begged him,
"Give her what she wants,
she is shouting at us,
she will never go away."
Jesus turned to the woman.
"Is it fair to take
the children's food
and throw it to their dogs?"
"Yes," she said,
"for the dogs eat the scraps
that fall from the family table."
Jesus responded,
"Great is your faith.
Be it done as you desire."
On arriving home,
she found her daughter in bed
and the demon gone.

◇ **Personal Reflection**

Schoolgirls
in colorful
cuts
of cloth
like a splash
of bougainvillea,
yet lovelier
to behold,
learning a new
sociology,
but returning

to the old.
What kind of world
lies ahead
for you,
my sisters,
called to be
saints?
A lifetime
of babies
at milk swollen
breasts
borne
with no complaints.
Remember
on days
of discouragement
your ancient
ancestry,
the life-giving force
that flows
in the veins
of matriarchal
society:
you have the power
within yourselves
to set
your sisters
free.

⬦ **Points for Shared Reflection**

- Consider the Canaanite woman as a role model for women today. She goes straight to Jesus to plead her case, until an all male hierarchy, prejudiced against her, ignores its law and comes around to supporting her request.

- Reflect on the mother-daughter bond and the extent to which a woman will go on behalf of the girlchild of her womb.

- Name some of the demons that torment young women in the world in which we live.

- Suppose the Canaanite family story was not really a case of demonic possession but one of a daughter's rebellion against a strong-willed mother which had resulted in an unmanageable child. Suppose the mother's encounter with Jesus and the exorcising of her own demons led to a more harmonious relationship with her daughter and to genuine healing in their home. Reflect on this interpretation of the miracle and the meaning it might have for you.

◇ **A Mother and Daughter Psalm** (see p. 88)

◇ **Prayer**

> O Nourishing, Nurturing,
> Mothering God,
> You know how much we love You.
> With You
> and through You
> and in You,
> we make our way back
> to the womb
> that gave birth
> to our bringing to birth
> on every level of living.
> May You never fail to feed us all
> with Your presence
> and Your promises,
> for from the beginning
> and always,
> we belong to You,
> we came from You,
> and to You we shall return.
> With joy we say: Amen!

———— ◇ ————

All   O Nourishing, Nurturing, Mothering God,
from our mother's womb You are our life:
You must know how much we love You.

Voice 1   Thank You, God, for this bundle of life
who was once a part of my body,
the focal point of my inner world,
the "I Am" of Your making,
whose struggle to be and become
someone
stretched the womb
of my being
until there was no more "I"
but "we,"
and the two of one flesh
became two in one spirit,
a never-to-be-broken bond.

Voice 2   Thank You, God, for this source of life
responsible for my growing,
in whom I lived
and moved
and had my being,
who shares the pangs
and understands
each bringing to birth
in me.

All   O Nourishing, Nurturing, Mothering God,
from our mother's womb You are our life:
You must know how much we love You.

Voice 1   Thank You, God, for this child of love
who feeds from the wellspring
within me,
who daily grows
more capable
of nourishing, nurturing me.

Voice 2   Thank You, God, for this mother-love
so full to overflowing,
whose breasts of compassion
comfort me
when the pull to move out and discover
pushes against the limits
of my finite capacity.

     By M. T. Winter, Crossroad Pub. Co., © 1990 Medical Mission Sisters

All   O Nourishing, Nurturing, Mothering God,
from our mother's womb You are our life:
You must know how much we love You.

Voice 1   Thank you, God, for this child of choice,
mirror of my meaning,
who shares my joys,
supports my views,
and never forgets
the little things
that matter so much to me.

Voice 2   Thank you, God, for this mother of mine,
gift of Your own giving,
who knows my needs,
who lets me go,
no matter how hard the leaving,
and who is always there for me.

All   O Nourishing, Nurturing, Mothering God,
from our mother's womb You are our life:
You must know how much we love You.

HERODIAS AND HER DAUGHTER

◇ **Scripture Reference**   Mark 6:17–29 / Matthew 14:3–12

◇ **Biography**

Herodias was living in adultery with Herod Antipas, who was the local ruler of Galilee and Perea and one of the sons of Herod the Great.
Both accounts identify her as the wife of Herod's brother, Philip, but
Josephus the historian, a reliable source, says she was the wife of another half brother who was also named Herod. According to Josephus,
the daughter of Herodias was named Salome, and it was she who was
married to Philip.

Herodias and her daughter are instrumental in the death of John the Baptist. The account of the execution is interpolated into both Gospel narratives and is obviously out of context. It is presented in the form of a flashback. In each of the Gospels a different point precipitates the remembering. For Mark it is the cost of discipleship inherent in the ministry. In Matthew it serves as an extended reflection on the words and the experience of Jesus about prophets not being accepted among those to whom they are well known.

◇ **Lectionary Reading**

Herod had imprisoned John
for the sake of Herodias,
his brother's wife,
with whom he had been living.
John had criticized Herod, saying,
"It is unlawful for you to have her."
His words angered both of them.
Herodias wanted to kill him.
But Herod feared John
and his many followers
who considered him a prophet.
On Herod's birthday
he threw a party,
inviting the courtiers
and officers
and the leaders of Galilee.
The daughter of Herodias danced,
and the men were so enchanted
that Herod beckoned to her and said,
"Because you have pleased me
and my guests,
ask for whatever you wish,
and I will give it to you."
Then he swore on an oath,
"Ask and I will give you
whatever you want,
even if it is half of my kingdom."
She went out to find her mother.
"What shall I ask for?"
Herodias said,
"The head of John the baptizer."
She hurried back to Herod.
"I want you to give me,
on a dish,
the head of John the Baptist."

Herod was shocked
and somewhat distressed.
However, he would not
break his oath.
To save face,
he gave in to the girl,
sent for a soldier of the guard
and ordered the execution.
John was beheaded in prison.
They put his head on a platter,
gave it to the girl,
and she gave it to her mother.
Later, John's disciples came
and buried the prophet's body.

◇ **Points for Shared Reflection**

• Reflect on the seductive influence of power and privilege. What happens when women are compromised by the perks of the ruling class?

• How does one break the cycle of evil that often passes from parent to child? Drugs, drink, promiscuity, depression, anxiety, fear, a negative sense of our own self worth — what are some of the consequences of such addictive behavior in society and in ourselves?

• Look closely at the women in this story. In what ways do we differ from Herodias and Salome and in what ways are we just like them?

• How responsible are the men for the outcome of this story?

• What do we do to the men whom we feel are standing in our way? Reflect on the Herodias syndrome lurking in us all.

◇ **A Psalm for Confronting Evil** (see p. 93)

◇ **Prayer**
O Warrior Woman,
You are our God
from the days of the earth's beginnings.
You guard Your precious charges
from the claws of all those predators
who seek to do us harm.
Slay those raging passions
that dehumanize and conquer,
and touch us all
with that gentleness
we need for making peace.
Gentle Woman God,
You are our God,
now and forever. Amen.

◇ A PSALM FOR CONFRONTING EVIL ◇

All   Deliver us from evil, O God,
in the world and in ourselves.

Choir 1   How can we be at peace within
when war is all around us
and our enemies prevail?

Choir 2   We fear the guns that shoot to kill
and all those slick theologies
that justify execution.

All   Deliver us from evil, O God,
in the world and in ourselves.

Choir 1   Where can we run to escape the rage
and violence
of our times?

Choir 2   We are victims who have been violated,
and we dare not deny
our wounds.

All   Deliver us from evil, O God,
in the world and in ourselves.

Choir 1   Be there when we are mistreated, O God,
by those who have power over us.

Choir 2   Help us empower each other in ways
that will help to transform us all.

All   Deliver us from evil, O God,
in the world and in ourselves.

Choir 1   Deliver us all from the evil inherent
in affluence
and domination.

Choir 2   Be with the poor as they struggle to rise
from the ghettoes of oppression,
destitution,
and despair.

All   Deliver us from evil, O God,
in the world and in ourselves.

Choir 1   Daily we are confronted by the evils
of drugs
and addiction,
the hypocrisy
of our leaders,
the ambivalence in ourselves.

By M. T. Winter, Crossroad Pub. Co., © 1990 Medical Mission Sisters   *WomanWord* / 93

Choir 2   Help us, O God, to be firm in faith
and fearless
in the face of evil,
to never lost heart
when confronted by
the harrowing hounds of hell.

All   Deliver us from evil, O God,
in the world and in ourselves.

—————— ◇ ——————

    By M. T. Winter, Crossroad Pub. Co., © 1990 Medical Mission Sisters

SALOME, MOTHER OF ZEBEDEE'S SONS

◇ **Scripture Reference**   Matthew 20:20–23; 27:55–56
Mark 15:40–41; 16:1

◇ **Biography**

Both Matthew and Mark mention Salome as one of the women who accompanied Jesus in Galilee, followed him to Jerusalem, and waited at the tomb with spices to anoint him after he died. Mark records her name (15:40; 16:1), but Matthew refers to her only as the mother of Zebedee's sons (20:20; 27:56). Her sons were James and John, whom Jesus called while they were in their boat mending nets with their father. He nicknamed them "sons of thunder."

John's account of the crucifixion lists the sister of the mother of Jesus among the women at the foot of the cross, leading some to speculate that this was Salome and that her sons and Jesus were cousins. While this would explain why Jesus handed his mother over to the care of John, and why John and his brother James, along with Peter, seemed to form a select circle among the Twelve, there is no tangible evidence to substantiate this claim.

Salome emerges from the shadows of Scripture when she comes to Jesus to ask him to reserve the choice places in the kingdom, at his right hand and his left, for her sons. Matthew alone hides the sons' quest for power behind the intervention of their mother. In Mark they plead their case themselves. What follows in both is a heated debate about who among them is the greatest, precipitating the response of Jesus indicating how those in authority must be like the least among them, like those who serve.

◇ **Lectionary Reading**

The mother of the sons of Zebedee
came to Jesus
accompanied by her sons.
Kneeling before him,
she requested a favor.
"What do you want?"
he asked her.
"That these sons of mine
may sit beside you,
one on your right hand
and one on your left,
when you are in your kingdom."
"You do not know what you are asking,"
he replied.
Turning to the two,
he inquired of them:
"Can you drink the cup
that I will drink?"
"Yes, we can,"
they answered.
"So be it," he said,
"you shall drink my cup,
but positions of power
to my right and my left
are not mine to give.
They are awarded by God
our Creator."

◇

There were many women at the tomb
who had followed Jesus from Galilee
where they had been accompanying him.
Among them were Mary Magdalene,
Mary the mother of James and Joseph,
and the mother of Zebedee's sons.

When the sabbath was over,
Mary Magdalene,
Mary the mother of James,
and Salome,
bought spices
for the anointing of Jesus.
Very early in the morning,
on the first day of the week,
just as the sun was rising,
the women went to the tomb.

◇ **Personal Reflection**

The round
moon
whispers:
why worry
about these things?
Reach
beyond
the momentary
anxiety
life brings,
to God
Who is rocking
rocking
rocking
the world
with Her wide
warm
welcoming
wings.

◇ **Points for Shared Reflection**

- Here we have a profile of a mother and her sons. Compare this story with two earlier stories of mothers and their daughters (pp. 84 and 90). What differences do you perceive?

- Salome is both aggressive and self-effacing. Her concern is for her sons. What are the learnings a mother might draw from this Gospel episode?

- Matthew never names the woman. He identifies her with a label resulting from her role. As a woman who has no doubt shared the experience, comment on this practice.

- What do you think was Salome's relationship to Jesus and what might have been her role in his ministry?

- Salome supports the custom of sons having to be number one. How does such a tradition hinder both male development and female equality in the world in which we live?

⋄ **A Mother's Psalm** (see p. 99)

⋄ **Prayer**

Godmother God,
Grandmother God,
this child of Your child
is Your offspring.
You are the source
and protection
of the life awakening here.
May You be present always
at the core of lighthearted laughter,
in the promise of unending years.
Together we praise You
and bless You,
now and forever.
Amen.

———— ⋄ ————

◇ A MOTHER'S PSALM ◇

All   Godmother God, raise this child
in the faith that supports Your promises.

Choir 1   I gave birth to a rose-fingered dawn
who touches my life with sunbeams,
reminding me,
when shadows fall,
that life does begin again.

Choir 2   I gave birth to a shooting star
who hurls across my horizon,
rising, falling,
filling my days
with spontaneity.

All   Godmother God, raise this child
in the faith that supports Your promises.

Choir 1   I gave birth to a summer day
who warms me
and fulfills me;
seed, bud, branch, bloom
will one day touch the sky.

Choir 2   I gave birth to thunder and rain,
to lightning flash
and fury,
whose sudden storms
are swift,
spawning rainbows
everywhere.

All   Godmother God, raise this child
in the faith that supports Your promises.

Choir 1   I gave birth to eagle's wings,
to one who craves the mountains,
seeking, soaring
high above mere
mediocrity.

Choir 2   I gave birth to a lion cub,
O God,
grant me this blessing,
that through this child's
graced leadership,
Your Word will rise again.

All   Godmother God, raise this child
in the faith that supports Your promises.

By M. T. Winter, Crossroad Pub. Co., © 1990 Medical Mission Sisters   *WomanWord* / 99

WOMAN IN THE CROWD

◇ **Scripture Reference**   Luke 11:27–28

◇ **Biography**

The woman is completely anonymous. She is simply a woman in the crowd.

◇ **Context**

The account of this incident is placed in the context of teaching about signs. The crowds around Jesus are increasing. Some were seeking a sign. They were looking for a miracle, but Jesus speaks of the word of God. He mentions Jonah and the queen of the south. Both had traveled a great distance, one to preach repentance, the other in search of wisdom. Matthew makes the sign of Jonah into a sign of the Resurrection. In Mark's account Jesus absolutely refuses even to speak of a sign. Luke is the only one who mentions the woman. She has missed the point of Jesus' mission in her brief, messianic confession. What matters is keeping the word of God. Those who do are blessed, and in an earlier passage are said to be part of Jesus' own family circle (8:21).

◇ **Lectionary Reading**

A woman in the crowd
surrounding Jesus
raised her voice

in benediction.
"Blessed is the womb that bore you.
Blessed are the breasts that nursed you."
Jesus contradicted her.
"Blessed rather
are those who hear the word of God
and keep it."

◇ **Personal Reflection**

Onyame
Bataan Pa,
good
Mother God,
nursing mother
God,
Holy
Wholly Other
Mystery
in Whom we live
and are set free:
reveal
Your secret name
to me
and with Your tender
midwifery,
reach within,
bring to birth
acknowledgment
of woman's worth,
and cradle
a fretful
infant
earth.

◇ **Points for Shared Reflection**

• Reflect on this passage in light of conflicting positions in our day concerning motherhood. What did Jesus really mean?

• This is a case where someone said the right thing at the wrong time and is therefore contradicted. Mention ways in which mothers can and do hear God's word and keep it.

• It took courage for this woman to preach her word. How does her experience relate to that of contemporary female preachers?

◇ **A Psalm for All Who Keep God's Word** (see p. 103)

◇ **Prayer**

O Word-made-Flesh,
refresh us all
who seek to do You justice.
Speak Your message loudly.
Help us discern Your word of truth
in the chaos all around us.
Help us to know Your messenger
in the midst of conflicting claims.
O Clear, Dear, Unequivocal Word,
as we hear one another into being,
help us to cherish each nuance
of Your presence in everyone.
O Word-made-Flesh,
we thank You
and we love You.
Amen.

———— ◇ ————

◇ **A PSALM FOR ALL WHO KEEP GOD'S WORD** ◇

All   Happy are we who are doers of the word,
who hear God's word
and keep it.

Voice 1   One thing alone does God require
and this do we seek to accomplish:
to do justice,
to love tenderly
to walk humbly
with our God.

All   Happy are we who are doers of the word,
who hear God's word
and keep it.

Voice 2   Who heals the brokenhearted
and binds the wounds of the oppressed,
feeds the hungry,
shelters the homeless,
sets the imprisoned free:
these are God's disciples,
God's family,
God's friends.

All   Happy are we who are doers of the word,
who hear God's word
and keep it.

Voice 3   The word of God is a two-edged sword
that cuts through all hypocrisy,
prunes the unsuspecting,
strikes at the root of evil,
pierces to the heart.

All   Happy are we who are doers of the word,
who hear God's word
and keep it.

Voice 4   The word of God is a lamp to our feet,
a lantern to our path,
the light of the world
crying out for a sign
of hope
and illumination.

All   Happy are we who are doers of the word,
who hear God's word
and keep it.

By M. T. Winter, Crossroad Pub. Co., © 1990 Medical Mission Sisters

Voice 5　The word of God is a spark of life
living among the rubble,
igniting a global consciousness
to ways we are one world only,
a beacon burning
deep in the hearts
of those who seek justice
and peace.

All　Happy are we who are doers of the word,
who hear God's word
and keep it.

Voice 6　The word of God is the Word made flesh
in every generation,
in the outcasts of the system,
on the margins of prestige and power,
on the downside of tradition,
in every face
and every place
where God's own Spirit dwells.

All　Happy are we who are doers of the word,
who hear God's word
and keep it.

Voice 7　Happy are all who love God's word
and live it to the full,
for they are like trees
by rippling streams,
birds that soar high
singing,
prophets of a new age
bringing
the good Good News
to all.

All　Happy are we who are doers of the word,
who hear God's word
and keep it.

　By M. T. Winter, Crossroad Pub. Co., © 1990 Medical Mission Sisters

WOMAN AT THE WELL

◇ **Scripture Reference** John 4:1–42

◇ **Biography**

The woman is a Samaritan from Sychar, a village not far from Jacob's Well. She has had five husbands. At the time she met Jesus, she was living with a man to whom she was not married.

◇ **Context**

Jesus was passing through Samaria, the most direct route from Judea to Galilee. Jews and Samaritans were bitterly estranged. They shared a common heritage, but for centuries had practiced different religions. Jesus pauses at Jacob's Well, which is located near Mount Gerizim, site of the Samaritan temple, and engages in a theological discourse with one who is triply despised: a woman, a Samaritan, a divorcée five times over who is currently living with another man. As he speaks of water and worship, she moves from a literal understanding to the level of metaphor and meaning.

While the disciples are upset at his breaking all the rules, she discerns a prophetic utterance and goes to witness to others regarding what she has seen and heard. The central teaching of the story focuses on living water as a symbol of God's vitality and wisdom. However, the theme of universal mission and the prediction concerning true worship being rooted in spirit and in truth should not be overlooked.

◇ **Lectionary Reading**

Jesus was passing through Samaria
on his way from Judea to Galilee.
Around midday,
he came to the village of Sychar,
which is near Jacob's Well.
Tired from traveling,
and thirsty,
he sat down beside the well.
He was alone,
for his disciples had gone ahead
into the village
to buy some food.
A woman came to draw water.
"Please, give me a drink," said Jesus.
"How can you, a Jew,
possibly ask me,
a Samaritan woman,
for a drink?"
For Jews were hostile to Samaritans.
"If you knew the gift of God," said Jesus,
"if you knew who it is
who is asking this of you,
you would have asked me
for a drink,
and I would have given you living water."
The woman replied,
"You have no bucket and the well is deep.
How will you get this life-giving water?
Are you greater than our ancestor Jacob
who gave us this well
and drank from it himself,
with his household
and his cattle?"
Jesus said,
"Whoever drinks the water

from Jacob's Well
will continue to thirst,
but whoever drinks the water
that I can give
will never thirst again;
for the water I give
becomes an inner spring
welling up to eternal life."
The woman said, "Sir,
give me this water,
that I may never again
have to draw from this well,
that I may never thirst again."

"Go and fetch your husband,"
Jesus said.
"I have no husband,"
the woman replied.
"Indeed you have no husband,"
he said,
"for you have had five husbands,
and now you are living with a man
to whom you are not married."
"You are a prophet,"
she said to him.
"Then explain this to me.
Our ancestors worshiped here
on this mountain,
yet your people say
that Jerusalem is the place
where people ought to worship."
"Believe me," said Jesus,
"the hour will come
when you will worship God
neither on this mountain
nor in Jerusalem.
The hour will come,
it is already here,
when true worshipers will worship God
in spirit and truth.
God is spirit,
and you must worship God
in spirit and truth."
She answered,
"I know the Messiah is coming,
the one who is called Christ,

it is he who will show us all things
when he comes."
Jesus said,
"I who am speaking to you,
I am he."

Just then his disciples returned,
and they were amazed
that he was speaking with a woman,
but none of them dared
to say to him,
"Why are you speaking with her?"
So the woman left her water jar
and hurried into the village
to spread the news,
telling people,
"Come, see a man
who has told me
everything I've done.
Can this man be the Christ?"
And they left the village
to come to him.

Meanwhile, the disciples
were urging him,
"Rabbi, please,
have something to eat."
But he replied,
"I have food to eat
you know nothing about."
They looked at one another.
"Who do you suppose
could have given him food?"
Jesus replied,
"My food is to do the will
of the One Who sent me,
to accomplish God's work.
Do you not say,
'there are four months
from sowing to harvest'?
Well I say,
look around you,
the fields are ripe for the harvest.
Already the reaper is compensated,
storing up for eternal life.
Both sower and reaper rejoice.
For it is said,

'One sows, another reaps.'
I sent you to reap what you have not sown.
You reap the rewards of their labor."

Many Samaritans from the village
believed in him
on the strength of the woman's testimony
that he revealed what she had not told.
They begged him to stay,
so he remained two days,
and many more believed
because of his word.
They said to the woman,
"We have heard for ourselves,
and we too believe
he is the savior of the world."

◇ **Personal Reflection**

Drink
drink deep
let it all
sink in
to the well
of your
remembering
and the spell
of your
imagining
against the day
after day
after day
devoid of time
to sit
and pray,
when your heart
is up against
the wall,
your thirsting spirit
will recall
what a blessing
so much time
and space is
and return you
to this
graced
oasis.

- Consider this story a turning point for women, then and now. Jesus ignores social prejudice and religious restrictions to entrust his word to a woman, one who is a foreigner and divorced, and reveals his true identity to her.

- The woman converses with Jesus, then leaves as soon as the disciples return. Her water jar is left behind. What do these ordinary actions say about women and women's way?

- Scripture clearly states that the woman preached Jesus and his word in Samaria. Reflect on this in light of ecclesiastical concerns about women in the priesthood or the pulpit.

- What do you think it means for us to worship in spirit and truth?

◇ **A Psalm on Living Water** (see p. 111)

◇ **Prayer**

Wellspring of Wisdom,
hear the cry
of Your faith-filled sons
and daughters,
whom Your sanctifying waters seek
to sooth
and satisfy.
We hunger
and thirst
for that life-giving word
hidden
in our tradition.
We are ready to risk all
gladly
as we struggle now
to worship You
in spirit
and truth.
Amen.

———— ◇ ————

◇ A PSALM ON LIVING WATER ◇

Leader   You are like a mountain spring,
           O Fountain of Living Water:

All   I sip from the deep down freshness
           of Your never-failing love.

Leader   You are like a summer rain,
           O Sudden Benediction:

All   drench my soul
           and quench my thirsting spirit
           with Your peace.

Leader   You are like a raging sea,
           O Storm Upon My Ocean:

All   breaking to bits
           my fragile bark
           as I learn to lean
           on You.

Leader   You are like a waterfall,
           Oasis in My Desert:

All   source of my heart's survival
           in the press
           and stress
           of life.

Leader   You are like a cleansing flood,
           River of Reconciliation:

All   washing away
           the selfish
           self-serving signs
           of my sinfulness.

Leader   You are like a bottomless well,
           O Cup of Lifegiving Water:

All   full up to overflowing.
           Praise be to You, Shaddai.

SISTERS OF JESUS

◇ **Scripture Reference**   Matthew 13:53–58 / Mark 6:1–6
                                  Matthew 12:46–50 / Mark 3:31–35

◇ **Biography**

No information on the sisters of Jesus survives except the reference to their existence recorded in both Matthew and Mark.

◇ **Context**

Since the fourth century there has been a tradition common to both Eastern and Western Christianity that the "brothers and sisters" of Jesus referred to his cousins (children of Mary's sister) or the children of Joseph from a previous marriage. Roman Catholicism insists on the perpetual virginity of Mary. Protestants generally do not share this view. Many proponents of the virgin birth, Catholic and Protestant, accept the fact that Mary and Joseph had other children, as implied in Matthew 1:24–25 and Luke 2:7. The synoptic narrative that tells about Jesus' return to his home village belongs to the early Jesus tradition and its implications regarding Jesus' female siblings cannot be so easily dismissed. Supporting this is biblical evidence and a well-established tradition that James, leader of the apostolic church in Jerusalem, was the brother of Jesus.

That so little is known about the sisters of Jesus is no surprise. That there has been such resistance to acknowledging his brothers, despite the evidence, reflects the strength of medieval developments favoring virginity and celibacy. Only his mother and brothers are mentioned in the biblical text of the second lection, yet Jesus clearly includes the word "sister" in his verbal response.

Since "brother" is still, for many, a term inclusive of both genders, we interpret it here to include the sisters of Jesus as well. Similarly, we can also assume that the sisters of Jesus were present at Pentecost with their mother and their brothers.

◇ **Lectionary Reading**

Jesus returned to Nazareth,
his hometown,
and taught in the synagogue
on the sabbath.
Those who heard him were astonished.
"Where did this man get his wisdom?
Isn't he the carpenter's son?
Isn't his mother the woman named Mary?
Aren't James and Joseph and Simon and Jude
his brothers?
Aren't all his sisters living here with us?
Then where did he get all this?"
They simply could not accept him.
And Jesus said to them:
"Prophets are only rejected
in their own neighborhood
and in their own house."
And he did not work many miracles there,
because they did not believe.

◇

While he was still speaking to the people,
his mother and his brothers and sisters arrived,
and they waited for him outside.
A messenger told him,
"Your mother and brothers and sisters
are here,
and they are asking for you."

Jesus said:
"Who are my mother
and my brothers
and my sisters?"
And looking at those all around him,
he said:
"Here are my mother
and my brothers
and my sisters!
Whoever does the will of God
is my brother
and my sister
and my mother."

◇ **Personal Reflection**

Why all the fuss?
Why couldn't it be
that God
Who made
both heaven
and planet earth
and you
and me
is one of us?

◇ **Points for Shared Reflection**

• The possibility of Jesus having sisters and brothers has long been suppressed. What do you think, and why?

• Leaving aside the question of the virgin birth of Jesus, what difference would it make to Christian spirituality today if Mary had borne other children? What have been some of the consequences of denying a sexual relationship between Mary and her husband Joseph?

• Imagine Jesus having siblings. Bring one of his sisters to life. What is she like? What does she think of her older brother and his unorthodox career? Weave her into one of the more familiar Gospel narratives or retell a Gospel story from her point of view.

◇ **A Psalm in Praise of Anonymous Women** (see p. 116)

◇ **Prayer**

O God of invisible women,
we have served You
all the days of our life
and still we do not know You,
called upon You,
worshiped You,
yet we still do not know
Your name.
So many miss the traces
of Your presence
here among us.
Invisible God
of invisible women,
to You be the praise
and glory,
now and forever.
Amen.

———— ◇ ————

◇ A PSALM IN PRAISE OF ANONYMOUS WOMEN ◇

Leader   For all those women unnamed and unknown
in the course of human history,
anonymous women,
invisible women,
unidentified and
unrecorded women,

All   we remember you now,
and we praise you.

Leader   Daughters and wives and mothers,
whose names are conspicuously missing
from the book of the generations:

All   Rejoice now as we praise you!

Leader   Daughters of Eve:

All   Rejoice now as we praise you!

Leader   Daughters and wife of Seth:

All   Rejoice now as we praise you!

Leader   Daughters and wife of Enosh:

All   Rejoice now as we praise you!

Leader   Daughters and wife of Kenan:

All   Rejoice now as we praise you!

Leader   Daughters and wife of Mahal'alel:

All   Rejoice now as we praise you!

Leader   Daughters and wife of Jared:

All   Rejoice now as we praise you!

Leader   Daughters and wife of Enoch:

All   Rejoice now as we praise you!

Leader   Daughters and wife of Methuselah:

All   Rejoice now as we praise you!

Leader   Daughters and wife of Lamech:

All   Rejoice now as we praise you!

Leader   Daughters and wife of Noah:

All   Rejoice now as we praise you!

Leader   All who were labeled "the daughters of men,"
who scripture says were taken to wife
by those who were labeled "the sons of God" —
may you and all your anonymous daughters:

 By M. T. Winter, Crossroad Pub. Co., © 1990 Medical Mission Sisters

All	Rejoice now as we praise you!
Leader	All anonymous women of the Hebrew scriptures:
All	Rejoice now as we praise you!
Leader	Daughters and wives and mothers whose names are unrecorded in the Gospels and writings of the early Church tradition:
All	Rejoice now as we praise you!
Leader	The mother of Mary the mother of Jesus:
All	Rejoice now as we praise you!
Leader	The sister of Mary the mother of Jesus:
All	Rejoice now as we praise you!
Leader	The sisters of their brother Jesus:
All	Rejoice now as we praise you!
Leader	Peter's mother-in-law:
All	Rejoice now as we praise you!
Leader	Woman accused of adultery:
All	Rejoice now as we praise you!
Leader	Widow from the village of Nain:
All	Rejoice now as we praise you!
Leader	Woman with the flow of blood:
All	Rejoice now as we praise you!
Leader	Jairus's little daughter:
All	Rejoice now as we praise you!
Leader	Woman who anointed the head of Jesus:
All	Rejoice now as we praise you!
Leader	Woman who anointed the feet of Jesus:
All	Rejoice now as we praise you!
Leader	Crippled woman bent over double:
All	Rejoice now as we praise you!
Leader	Poor widow who generously gave away all:
All	Rejoice now as we praise you!
Leader	Canaanite woman and her daughter:
All	Rejoice now as we praise you!
Leader	Anonymous woman in the crowd:
All	Rejoice now as we praise you!

By M. T. Winter, Crossroad Pub. Co., © 1990 Medical Mission Sisters

Leader	Samaritan woman at the well:
All	Rejoice now as we praise you!
Leader	Wife of Pontius Pilate:
All	Rejoice now as we praise you!
Leader	Maid in the house of Caiaphas, the high priest:
All	Rejoice now as we praise you!
Leader	Galilean women who accompanied Jesus:
All	Rejoice now as we praise you!
Leader	Weeping daughters of Jerusalem:
All	Rejoice now as we praise you!
Leader	Women in the Upper Room at Pentecost:
All	Rejoice now as we praise you!
Leader	Women persecuted by Saul:
All	Rejoice now as we praise you!
Leader	Women who were members of the apostolic church:
All	Rejoice now as we praise you!
Leader	Female slave in Philippi:
All	Rejoice now as we praise you!
Leader	Four female prophets, daughters of Philip the evangelist:
All	Rejoice now as we praise you!
Leader	Paul's sister who lived in Rome:
All	Rejoice now as we praise you!
Leader	Mother of Rufus who lived in Rome:
All	Rejoice now as we praise you!
Leader	Sister of Nereus who lived in Rome:
All	Rejoice now as we praise you!
Leader	All anonymous women in the early church and throughout Christian history, up to and including today:
All	Rejoice now as we praise you!
Leader	Anonymous women everywhere, of every culture and every class, every religion and every race, from the beginning of time to this time and place, especially those who are in our midst:
All	Rejoice now as we praise you!

   By M. T. Winter, Crossroad Pub. Co., © 1990 Medical Mission Sisters

MARY'S SISTER

◇ **Scripture Reference**   John 19:25

◇ **Biography**

We meet Mary's sister for the first and only time in John's list of women who stood at the foot of the cross. Among the four women are the mother of Jesus and "his mother's sister." That is all we know of her.

◇ **Context**

Little is written of Mary's sister. Those commentaries that include her take her existence for granted as premise for explaining the scriptural references to "the brothers and sisters of Jesus." They conclude that these passages do not refer to Mary's children, the siblings of Jesus, but rather to the children of Mary's sister who are therefore cousins to Jesus. The inclusion of Mary's sister in the select circle at the foot of the cross may well be the Gospel writer's way of saying yet another time that those called to discipleship, specifically Johannine discipleship, are people close to Jesus. Whether or not they are family members, all who truly love and are loved by Jesus become one family in Christ.

◇ **Lectionary Reading**

Standing by the cross of Jesus
were Mary his mother,
her sister,
Mary the wife of Clopas,
and Mary Magdalene.

◇ **Personal Reflection**

Across the void
the violence
of those goodbyes
I relive
with regret
even yet
no interruption
no interim ties
can make me forget
the tilt of your face
the haunting
embrace
of your eyes.

◇ **Points for Shared Reflection**

• What might Mary have shared with her sister? Would she have told her of the circumstances surrounding the conception of Jesus? What do you share with your sister, or would you share if you had one, or if you could?

• Select an incident in the life of Mary and reflect on it from the perspective of Mary's sister. Or join with another person and each of you assume the role of one of the sisters. Share your insights within your larger woman circle.

• Reflect on the meaning of "sister" and "sisterhood" within the black community, among congregations of women religious in Roman Catholicism, and as indicative of the bond of solidarity linking all women. Who are the women whom you call "sister"?

• Since the early centuries, women in the church have been referred to generically as "brothers." How do you feel about this? What steps are you prepared to take to ensure that the term "sisters" is added to the language of scripture and its interpretation and to liturgical ritual and its implementation?

◇ **A Psalm for My Sisters** (see p. 122)

◇ **Prayer**

O Sensitive Spirit,
Sister Spirit,
You inhabit my soul
and the soul of my sisters.
Be the bond that binds us together
through the tough times
of our liberation.
Be the Spirit of solidarity
at the heart of our global spirit.
Make us one
in one another
through the unity of Your presence
in all the varied prayers and practices
of our graced diversity.
Fill us, fulfill us,
and free us
from all that hurts or hinders
Your free-flowing force within us.
Come, Sister Spirit,
be with us all,
now and forever.
Amen.

———— ◇ ————

Voice 1   I sing of you, my sisters,
a song of the Serengeti,
a song of your Ashanti mammies
before you were enslaved,
a song of the rain-swollen river
rising
and falling
like tribal hopes
or the cadence of drums
or the full-bodied dance
of the festival of yams;
for you are black and beautiful,
wise with the wisdom of mountains,
warm as the equatorial sun,
laden with wealth asleep on your back,
full to the brim with enough to nurture
the future
that clings
to your round black breast.

Voice 2   I sing of you, my sisters,
a song of bamboo forests,
a song of an early morning monsoon
with rhythms ringing
from the corrugated tin
of roof and spout and barrel;
for you are oriental
and open
to the mysticism of millennia,
channeling all the power and truth
that arises
in the East
to oases of the spirit,
weaving the thin threads
of planet earth
to the web
of ancient sophistry
through tapestries
of stars.

Voice 3   I sing of you, my sisters,
a song of the chaotic carnival,
a song of the mariachi,
of maracas
and castanets,

   By M. T. Winter, Crossroad Pub. Co., © 1990 Medical Mission Sisters

a song of all those intent on surviving
the hot blasts of oppression
with spirit
and with class;
for you are hispanic and full of life
and laughter
and love
and longing,
a fire on the mountain,
awaiting new growth
in the stark, starless night
of poverty,
a firefly,
strong as an Amazon warrior,
proud as the primeval rain forest
and as precious
to us all.

Voice 4   I sing of you, my sisters,
a song of caves and volcanic rock,
a song of the hoop and the circle,
a song of the village campfire
and those circles
within circles
spiraling back
to the dawn of time;
for you are black and brown and red,
you are Aborigine,
indigenous,
the first to name
and claim
the earth,
you rose up in the dreamtime
in solidarity with your sisters —
witchity grubs
and honey-ants
out back
of civilization —
and traced the paths of their songlines
and yours
into our history;
you walked the red road
of clay
and blood,
aware that all six directions
lead us into

the Mystery,
that the vision, the dream,
Great Spirit, Shaddai
are inseparable
and we are one.

All   I sing to you, my sisters,
a crescendoing song of freedom
from apartheid
in all its
hideous forms;
from the sacrilege
of Tiananmen Square
and the bloodbath
of Cambodia;
from the slaughter of your cosmic truth
by those who invade
your integrity
in the present
as well as the past;
from the pain of lost opportunity
in the ghettoes
of our cities,
the raping of your future,
the denial of your heritage
both north and south
of the border,
the enforced captivity
of sister-soul
and fun-loving
sister-spirit.

Voices   I sing of you, my sisters,
a song of sisterhood,
of global sisterhood,
of cosmic sisterhood,
of sisterly love
for you.

All   I sing of all that you've been,
and are,
and of all that you will be,
and I pray that one day,
my sisters,
you will sing a song
of me.

MARTHA AND MARY

◇ **Scripture Reference**   Luke 10:38–42

◇ **Biography**

Martha and Mary were sisters who lived with their brother Lazarus in Bethany, a village outside Jerusalem. John writes that "Jesus loved Martha and her sister and Lazarus" (11:5). Martha was practical, the mistress of the house, while Mary was more contemplative. Jesus wept at the death of their brother whom he raised again to life. The Gospels record three separate occasions when Jesus was a guest in their home.

◇ **Context**

The pericope of Martha and Mary is situated between a parable on service (Good Samaritan) and a teaching on prayer (Lord's Prayer) and seems constructed to be a bridge between the two. Martha's concern

125

about serving and Mary's silent attentiveness to Jesus have sparked debates contrasting the essentials of hospitality and genuine service with the importance of putting God first. Elisabeth Schüssler Fiorenza makes a strong case for seeing Martha's table service as a symbol of eucharistic ministry (see *In Memory of Her*, p. 165). Elsewhere she suggests that the rebuke to Martha in her presiding role and the affirmation of Mary's silent compliance may have been an attempt by the patriarchal church to put women back in their place. Luke's historical facts differ from those of John. According to John, the sisters live in Bethany and are close friends of Jesus. According to Luke their village is either in Samaria or Galilee and their relationship to Jesus is less clearly defined.

◇ **Lectionary Reading**

In the course of his journey
Jesus came to a village
where a woman named Martha
invited him to her home.
Her sister Mary
sat at his feet,
completely absorbed
in his teaching.
Martha, overwhelmed
with preparing the food,
complained to Jesus, saying:
"Do you not care
that my sister has left me
to serve you by myself?
Tell her, please, to help me."
"Martha, Martha,"
Jesus replied,
"you are anxious and fretful
about too many things.
One thing alone is essential.
Mary has chosen wisely.
There is no need for her to change."

◇ **Personal Reflection**

Jesus,
did you ever
feel
the fierce force
the push
the pull
of days
and nights
that were far

too full
of people
and programs
you thought
willed
by One
Whose way
must be
fulfilled?
When
at the end
of a difficult
day
with barely time
to pause
and pray
before the crowds
began to press
upon you,
did you
also bless
each God-given
opportunity?
If so,
Jesus,
remember me.

◇ **Points for Shared Reflection**

- With whom in this passage do you particularly identify and why?

- Luke casts his story in a patriarchal frame. The sisters are in competition, there are hierarchies of need, value, choice. Given what you know of the characters and circumstances, how might a woman have related the event?

- Which of the sisters might be a role model for today's feminist, and why?

- Even dedicated feminists are sometimes in competition with one another. Was there ever a time when you too felt constrained by a sister or envious of her?

- "One thing alone is essential." What do you think that is? Is what is essential more compatible with any particular role?

- The female images embedded in this story are not particularly attractive: frenetic or withdrawn, a workaholic or one who is insensitive to stress. What other images, negative or positive, can you discover here?

- Reflect on the tension between women's roles, both in religion and society. Look at the text from the perspective of one who is primarily a homemaker, then as one who has chosen a career. What is your own perspective? What does this story say to you?

◇

◇ **Scripture Reference**   John 11:1–45

◇ **Context**

The following story unfolds on two levels, the factual and the symbolic. The brother of Martha and Mary dies. Jesus, after some delay, raises him from the dead. This third resurrection story recorded in the Gospels also involves women (see Widow of Nain, p. 53; Jairus's Daughter, 62). Once again Jesus reveals his secret identity to a woman. Martha's Christological confession mirrors that of Peter at Caesarea Philippi (Mt 16:16). The personalities of the two sisters are developed more fully here.

◇ **Lectionary Reading**

Lazarus of Bethany was ill.
His sisters, Martha and Mary,
sent this message to Jesus.
"The man you love is ill."
On receiving the message,
Jesus said,
"This sickness will not end in death.
It is for the glory of God
and for the anointed one's glorification."

Now Jesus loved Martha
and Mary
and Lazarus,
yet when he learned
that Lazarus was ill,
he delayed two days
before saying to his disciples,
"Let us return to Judea."
"Rabbi," they said,
"why go back?
The last time they tried to stone you."
"Are there not twelve hours of daylight?"
he asked. Then he said:
"Who walks by day does not stumble,
because there is light to see by.
Whoever walks at night, stumbles,
for there is no guiding light.
Our friend Lazarus is sleeping,
and I am going now to wake him."
The disciples replied,

"If he sleeps, he will recover."
They misunderstood what Jesus meant,
so then he told them plainly:
"Lazarus is dead.
I am glad, for your sake,
that I was not there,
because now you will become a believer.
So let us go to him."
Thomas, the Twin, said to the others,
"Let us go and die with him."

When Jesus arrived,
he learned that Lazarus
had been in the tomb four days.
Now Bethany is only two miles from Jerusalem,
and many had come to sympathize
and remain with Martha and Mary.
When Martha heard that Jesus had come,
she went outside to meet him,
while Mary remained in the house.
Martha said to Jesus:
"If you had been here,
he would not have died.
Yet I know
that whatever you ask
from God,
God will give to you."
Jesus said to her,
"Your brother will rise again."
Martha said,
"I know he will rise again
at the final resurrection."
Then Jesus said:
"I am the resurrection
and the life;
who believes in me,
though dead,
shall live,
who lives
and believes in me
shall never die.
Do you believe this?"
"Yes," she said,
"I believe you are the Christ,
the anointed of God,
who has come into the world."

After saying this,
Martha went to call her sister Mary.
"He is here," she whispered,
"he is asking for you."
Hearing this, Mary got up
and went with haste to meet him.
Since he was still at a distance,
those who were with Mary in the house
thought she had gone to the tomb to weep,
so they hurried after her.
On reaching Jesus,
she fell at his feet, crying,
"If you had been here,
he would not have died."
At the sight of her tears,
and the tears of her friends,
Jesus was overcome.
"Where have you put him?"
he asked with anguish.
They answered,
"Come and see."
And with that,
Jesus wept.
Many who were present
said to one another,
"See how much he loved him."
But some remarked,
"Couldn't he who opened the eyes
of the blind man
have saved this man from dying?"

Still grieving,
Jesus reached the tomb,
a cave with a stone before it.
"Roll away the stone," he said,
but Martha tried to prevent it.
"He has been dead four days," she argued,
"the stench will be appalling."
But Jesus insisted.
"Have I not told you,
that if you believe,
you will see the glory of God?"
So they removed the stone.
Jesus, raising his eyes, prayed,
"My God, I thank you for hearing my prayer.

Indeed, you always hear me;
but I speak for the sake of those
who are here,
that they may believe you sent me."
Then he shouted loudly,
"Lazarus, come out."
The dead man came out.
His hands were bound,
his feet were bound,
his face had a cloth wrapped around it.
"Unwrap him and set him free,"
said Jesus.
And many of those
who had come to mourn
and had witnessed this deed,
now believed in him.

◇ **Points for Shared Reflection**

- Jesus expresses a range of emotions in the context of this narrative: grief, tears, friendship, love. Three times we are told how much he loved the family at Bethany. How do you feel knowing that Jesus was in touch with and shared such feelings?

- To which of the sisters do you feel particularly drawn, and why?

- Why do you think Jesus continually chooses a woman to whom to reveal the innermost part of his being?

- In the first reading Martha presides at table, in the second, her Christological confession mirrors that of Peter. In both narratives, she is clearly a leader. What implications do you draw from this?

- Compare the resurrection narratives recorded in the Gospels (Widow of Nain; Jairus's Daughter; Lazarus; Jesus) and the role of women in them. What applications might you draw from this reflection?

◇

◇ **Scripture Reference**   John 12:1–8

◇ **Context**

This anointing story has been confused with similar events recorded in the Synoptic Gospels (see "Context," pp. 66 and 71). Here Mary of Bethany anoints Jesus. Her story is unique to John.

◇ **Lectionary Reading**

Six days before the Passover,
Jesus was invited to Bethany for a meal.
Lazarus was there,
whom he had raised from the dead.

Martha served,
while Lazarus was among those
who were at the table.
Mary took a pound of costly ointment
and anointed the feet of Jesus
and wiped them with her hair.
The house was filled
with its fragrance.
But Judas Iscariot,
one of his disciples,
the one who was soon to betray him, said,
"Why wasn't this ointment sold
for three hundred denarii
and the money given to the poor?"
Not that he cared about the poor.
He said this because he was a thief.
Judas was in charge of the common fund,
and he would help himself to the money.
"Let her alone," Jesus said,
"she has kept this perfume for my burial.
The poor you have with you always.
You will not always have me."

⬧ **Points for Shared Reflection**

- In all three readings in which Mary of Bethany appears, we find her at the feet of Jesus. What do you suppose this means?

- Compare the three anointing narratives, the women, their actions, the settings, the dialogue. (See "Lectionary Reading," pp. 67 and 71.) Note similarities and differences. What does this comparison suggest?

- Discuss the dialogue concerning the poor. How would you interpret the words of Jesus?

- The men sat at table while the women provided some form of service for them. How do you feel about that? What would you say to Lazarus, the host, newly risen from the dead?

⬧ **A Psalm of Love** (see p. 134)

◇ **Prayer**

O Love That Lives Forever,
You carry the one You call
to follow You,
lifting her high
and higher,
until her will no longer lives
except to live in You.
Increase our capacity for love.
May we mirror Your own loving.
May we love the whole of Your universe
in the way that we love You.
With love we say:
Amen.

———— ◇ ————

◇ A PSALM OF LOVE ◇

Choir 1   I love you, O God, with all my heart,
and with the whole
of my being.

Choir 2   Wide open am I to love
and be loved
because You have first
loved me.

Choir 1   Daily I seek to share that love
as I touch the lives
of others.

Choir 2   Daily I see and receive that love
as others reach out
to me.

Choir 1   Teach me to serve you
generously
as a sign of love
extended.

Choir 2   Teach me to sit at the feet
of Your Word
made love
in history.

Choir 1   Your love is a friend who is there
for me
in the silence of
my mourning.

Choir 2   Your love is a resurrected hope
to one well beyond
surprise.

Choir 1   Love grows greater by loving
You
and loving
one another.

Choir 2   Love grows bigger and better
by living
the love
that never dies.

 By M. T. Winter, Crossroad Pub. Co., © 1990 Medical Mission Sisters

PILATE'S WIFE

◇ **Scripture Reference**   Matthew 27:15–26

◇ **Biography**

Pilate's wife, a Gentile woman, had a dream and took it seriously. That is all we know of her.

◇ **Context**

Pilate, procurator of Judea, was the only one who had the authority to pronounce the sentence of death. When Jesus is brought before him, Pilate's wife intercedes on his behalf. All four Gospels indicate that Pilate did not think Jesus was guilty and that he tried to release him. In the synoptic accounts he offers Barabbas as a substitute. The image of Pilate that emerges from these narratives differs from the ruthless characterization chronicled in the works of Philo and Josephus and in a single sentence of Luke (13:1). Two developments are unique to Matthew's record of the trial: the warning by Pilate's wife, and Pilate's washing his hands of any guilt regarding the death of Jesus. The historical validity of his wife's warning is suspect, as the dream motif appears elsewhere in Matthew (1:20; 2:12, 13, 19). However, it is entirely possible that it happened as recorded here.

While he was sitting in judgment on Jesus,
Pilate's wife sent a message to her husband.
"Have nothing to do with that innocent man.
I have been upset all day
because of a dream I had about him."
Now at festival time
it was customary for the governor
to release a prisoner to the people,
anyone they wanted.
There was in custody at the time
a notorious prisoner named Barabbas.
So when the crowd assembled,
Pilate asked them,
"Whom do you want me to release to you,
Barabbas or Jesus
who is called Christ?"
Pilate knew they had handed Jesus over
out of envy.
But the chief priests and elders
persuaded the people
to choose Barabbas
instead of Jesus.
Pilate asked them,
"Which of the two
shall I release to you?"
The crowd cried out,
"Barabbas!"
"Then tell me,"
said Pilate,
"what am I to do with Jesus
who is called Christ?"
They cried out,
"Crucify him!"
"Why?" asked Pilate.
"What harm has he done?"
But they shouted all the louder:
"Let him be crucified!"
When Pilate saw that he had no choice,
that in fact a riot was imminent,
he took some water
and washed his hands,
saying in front of the people:
"I am innocent of the blood of this man.
The responsibility is yours."

Then he released Barabbas,
had Jesus scourged,
and ordered his crucifixion.

◇ **Personal Reflection**

I saw
sun thaw
three little ice-crusted
branches,
warm form
puddles
from droplets
doing some
delicate dances.
I felt
rage melt
giving us all
second chances.

◇ **Points for Shared Reflection**

- Pilate's wife remains invisible, hidden behind a man. On the basis of an intuition, she intervenes with a plea for justice, but patriarchy prevails. Compare her experience to the experiences of women today, perhaps even your own.

- As you reflect on her story, do you think Pilate's wife had any influence on her husband? If so, in what way?

- Reflect on the fact that Jesus once again revealed his real self to a woman, once again to a foreigner, this time of the privileged class.

- Because of her political and social status, Pilate's wife would be classified as an oppressor, yet in what ways might it be legitimate to consider her also among the oppressed?

◇ **A Liberation Psalm for Women** (see p. 138)

◇ **Prayer**

O Liberating God,
O Pledge of Freedom,
You spoke Your Word on behalf of women,
calling each of us by name
to participate in your mission.
You go before us preparing the way
through fury, flood, and fire.
Be with us as we live our lives
in Your liberating love. Amen.

———   ◇   ———

All   Where shall we find a liberated woman?
In the public square,
in the corridors of power,
in the pulpits,
and in our midst.

Choir 1   She dares to stand up for freedom,
not only for her gender,
but for all who are oppressed.

Choir 2   Challenging those who oppose her,
she puts her hand to systemic change,
knowing that only time will tell
how effective are her ways.

Choir 1   If married, she is a wholesome wife
who loves and supports her husband,
yet has a life of her own,
a separate identity,
personal plans and goals.

Choir 2   If single, she has a sense of self
and rock solid relationships
that nourish and enrich her
and help to make her whole.

Choir 1   If permanently bound to another
in a covenant of love,
she seeks to share
her inner strength
and vision
with the world.

Choir 2   She shares herself with all who hunger
for meaning
and for love,
sinking her roots
in a rich and personal experience
of her God.

All   Who is the strength of a liberated woman?
Her God,
her family,
her friends,
for she grows by their affirmation
and succeeds through support
and a helping hand,
all the days of her life. Amen.
Yes, let us say: Amen!

    By M. T. Winter, Crossroad Pub. Co., © 1990 Medical Mission Sisters

HIGH PRIEST'S MAID

◇ **Scripture Reference**   Mark 14:66–72 / Matthew 26:69–75
Luke 22:54–62 / John 18:15–17

◇ **Biography**

The woman is a maid in the home of Caiaphas, the high priest. Nothing more is known of her.

◇ **Context**

Jesus has been apprehended and is brought before the Jewish authorities who have assembled at the home of the high priest, sometime between midnight and dawn. As they put him on trial, his disciples are milling around in the outer courtyard, trying to remain inconspicuous. One of the maids suspects Peter's identity, but he denies any association with Jesus and his disciples.

◇ **Lectionary Reading**

One of the maids of the high priest
saw Peter in the courtyard,
warming himself by the fire.
"You were also with Jesus the Nazarene,"
she said.
But Peter vehemently denied it.
"I have no idea what you mean."

139

The maid saw him later again
on the porch
and began to say to the bystanders,
"This man is one of them."
But again Peter denied it.
Eventually the bystanders said to Peter,
"Surely you are one of their company,
for your accent is Galilean."
But he began to curse and swear
and answered with an oath:
"I do not know this man."
A cock crowed,
and Peter remembered.
"Before a cock crows twice,"
he had been warned by Jesus,
"three times you will deny me."
And Peter broke down
and wept.

⬦ **Personal Reflection**

Thirty pieces
of silver
fish,
the price
of poverty:
oppressors
sell
the offspring
of God
through a captive
economy,
while the guilty —
is it I,
my Lord? —
cultivate
piety.

⬦ **Points for Shared Reflection**

- A future leader of the church lies and denies all association with Jesus, then sees his sin and repents. Bishops have admitted that the sin of sexism resides in the Catholic church. What are some of the denials associated with this sin? What are some forms of repentance?

- A female servant calls a member of the hierarchy to accountability. In light of the words of Jesus concerning the least and the greatest among us, reflect on the woman's word of truth in the face of Peter's lie, her position in light of his status, her honesty and his response.

- As a servant bound by loyalty, do you think the maid might have been questioning Peter's abandonment of his master and not just exposing his identity?
- Recall from memory the Passion narratives describing the suffering and death of Jesus. Name the women who appear. What roles do they play? In the same way, reflect on the men.

◇ **A Psalm of Integrity** (see p. 142)

◇ **Prayer**

Deliver us, O God,
from any hesitation
to take a stand for justice.
May we never run
from our responsibility
to You.
In You, O God,
we find the strength
to confront the forces of evil,
the courage to stand firm
and speak Your truth
no matter what the cost.
You are our way,
our truth, our life,
our integrity forever.
Holy are You,
O Blessed Indwelling,
now and forever.
Amen.

——— ◇ ———

◇ A PSALM OF INTEGRITY ◇

Choir 1   O God, be my integrity
in the midst of lies
and in all the deceitful practices
that abound.

Choir 2   Shield me from the dishonesty
that permeates our culture
and pervades the halls of power.

Choir 1   Let me speak Your truth unflinchingly
aloud
in public places.

Choir 2   Let me call to accountability
all those who claim to keep Your word
yet violate our trust.

Choir 1   In the rites of life
and religion,
may I never turn to other gods
or empty ritual making.

Choir 2   In all my daily dealings,
may I never trade
on pretense
or make outlandish claims,
or hide behind
the flimsy veil
of a false humility.

Choir 1   May I never deny Your grace in me
or credit other sources.

Choir 2   May I never forget that a lust for power
pinned You to a cross.

Choir 1   Deliver us all from a public ethic
divorced from private practice.

Choir 2   Lead us, O God, to confess our failings,
to seek and ask forgiveness,
and help us begin again.

      By M. T. Winter, Crossroad Pub. Co., © 1990 Medical Mission Sisters

DAUGHTERS OF JERUSALEM

◇ **Scripture Reference**   Luke 23:26–31

◇ **Biography**

An unspecified number of women followed Jesus to the place of crucifixion, weeping and lamenting. Some may have been disciples, some
may have been believers, some may have heard him speak in the past
or heard others speak of him. Among the women who were residents
of Jerusalem were surely those Galilean women who had come up to
the city with Jesus and who remained with him as he suffered, died,
and was buried.

As Jesus was led away to be crucified, he was followed by women keening a death-wail in anticipation of his fate. To publicly lament the execution of someone condemned by the authorities was an act of uncommon courage. Jesus turns and addresses the women. The phrase "daughters of Jerusalem" functions metaphorically here, for Jesus warns them that what is happening to him will happen to all of Jerusalem and will affect the course of their own lives. The evil of the present moment will spill over into the next generation. To be childless will be considered a blessing, not a curse. Weep because of this, he tells the women, "weep for yourselves and for your children."

◇ **Lectionary Reading**

As they led Jesus away,
they seized Simon of Cyrene,
a man who had come in from the country,
and forced him to take the cross from Jesus
and carry it behind him.
There followed a multitude of people,
among them women who beat their breasts
and wept and wailed for him.
Jesus turning to them said,
"Daughters of Jerusalem,
do not weep for me,
but weep for yourselves
and for your children.
For the days are coming when people will say,
'Blessed are those who are childless,
blessed are the wombs that have never given birth
and the breasts that have never nursed.'
Then they will say to the mountains,
'Fall on us,' and to the hills,
'Cover us up!'
For if this is what they do
when the wood is green,
what will happen when the wood is dry?"

◇ **Personal Reflection**

The shrill screams
of a frightened child
pierce the humid air
of Nong Chan camp
this sultry morning.
Situation Zero,
says Bravo security.
It's safe now.

Nothing to fear.
Explain to the child here
in OPD
that the distant shelling
has dissipated,
that the troops amassed
behind the hills
ready to strike
are quiet now
and there's nothing to fear,
nothing to fear.
Rain inundates
the landscape
with its tensions
and its tears,
seeking to sooth
the wounds of war:
Cambodia
mourning
her children's
children
because they are
no more.

◇ **Points for Shared Reflection**

• Women of Jerusalem wept at the injustice about to occur. Injustice still prevails. What injustices do you mourn?

• Women wept at the loss of an innocent life. The present age is characterized by a loss of innocence. What lost innocence do you mourn?

• Women wept at the impending execution of Jesus. Human beings are still being executed. Does this fact cause you to mourn?

• Women, we were told to weep for ourselves. What is it about your life, past or present, that causes you to weep?

• Women, we were told to weep for our children. What is it about your children, or the children of the world, that causes you to weep?

◇ **A Psalm for Women Who Weep** (see p. 147)

◇ **Prayer**

We turn to You,
God of the One Who wept
for Lazarus
and Jerusalem.
We turn to You,
God Who surely wept
at the death
of Jesus the Christ.
You are a God
Who has felt the loss
of a child, a people, a friend.
Weep with us who weep for our own
unrealized potential
and promises unfulfilled.
Weep with women learning to weep
at the hideous crucifixion
of their own giftedness.
Weep for the children
of weeping children,
for the little girl lost
in a hostile world
or a woman's hardened heart.
Weep with us, for us, in us,
as we struggle through pain
toward a new tomorrow
when we will weep no more.
O God, Refuge of all who weep,
we turn to You.
Amen.

———— ◇ ————

◇ A PSALM FOR WOMEN WHO WEEP ◇

Leader	Women, why do we weep?
All	We weep for the slaughter of innocence, for the death of God in a secular world, for the crucifixion of hope. We weep:
Choir 1	for children of the holocaust, for sisters sold into slavery, for women strung out on drugs,
Choir 2	for the damning of the goddess, for the condemning of unauthorized goodness, for the killing of soul and spirit under the weight of a heavy cross.
Leader	Women, why do we weep?
All	We weep for all our children, for the children of our children, for the child within us all. We weep:
Choir 1	for babies born of addicted mothers, for children bearing the scars of abuse, for children who feel alone and unloved,
Choir 2	for children with children, too old, too young, for children who are disadvantaged, for children who have known only war.
Leader	Women, why do we weep?
All	We weep for ourselves, yes, for ourselves and all the misunderstandings that have circumscribed our lives. We weep:
Choir 1	for graces we have forfeited, for capabilities untested, for affirmation denied,
Choir 2	for deaths without resurrection, for pain with no justification, for hungers unsatisfied.
Leader	Women, why do we weep?
Choir 1	We weep because the whole world is weeping as another generation dies.
Choir 2	We weep because our beloved earth looks back at us, and cries.

By M. T. Winter, Crossroad Pub. Co., © 1990 Medical Mission Sisters   *WomanWord* / 147

WOMEN WHO ACCOMPANIED JESUS

◇ **Scripture Reference**   Luke 8:1–3

Mark 15:40–41, 47; 16:1–11
Matthew 27:55–56, 61; 28:1–10
Luke 23:49, 55–56; 24:1–25
John 19:25; 20:1–18

◇ **Biography**

All four Gospels attest to the fact that women accompanied Jesus in ministry. Several we know by name: Mary of Magdala; Mary the mother of James the younger and of Joseph; Joanna, the wife of Chuza, Herod's steward; Salome, the mother of Zebedee's sons; and Susanna. At the foot of the cross we also meet Mary the wife of Clopas, and the sister of the mother of Jesus. Many other women also journeyed with Jesus, a fact clearly stated in the texts. These women were Galilean, at least some of them were well-to-do, and some were related to the apostles or other disciples. Luke adds that the women who followed Jesus were those who had been healed of demonic possession or other serious illnesses. There is some identity confusion involving those women named Mary, a name that recurs throughout the New Testament accounts concerning Jesus, and in those that record the development of the church.

◇ **Context**

Mark continually distinguishes between the twelve and the wider circle of disciples who also have been called. The twelve are men, identified by name, but there is no reason to assume that the others are necessarily male. He uses three verbs to describe the discipleship of the Galilean women. They "follow" Jesus, "minister" to him, and they "came up with him" to Jerusalem. The phrase "came up with him" is used only once more in the New Testament, where it refers to those who had encountered the resurrected Lord and were his witnesses (Acts 13:31).

The precise nature of the women's contribution in ministry is uncertain. According to Luke, they provided material assistance to Jesus and the twelve. The nature of their commitment, however, is clear from the texts concerning the final days of Jesus. Male apostles betrayed, denied, and abandoned Jesus in order to protect themselves, while female disciples risked their lives to be with him on the way to his death, at the cross, and at the tomb. Consequently, they were the ones who were witnesses to the fact of his resurrection, the ones to whom the risen Christ entrusted his first word.

Several conflicting traditions are preserved concerning the facts of Easter morning. John records that Mary Magdalene went to the tomb and she alone conveyed the news of the empty chamber to the apostles. Matthew refers to Mary Magdalene and the other Mary; Mark says it was Mary Magdalene, Mary the mother of James, and Salome; Luke substitutes Joanna for Salome. In Matthew and Luke the women run to inform the apostles. There is no mention in Matthew of their disbelief. In Mark the women remain silent, "because they were afraid." In John, only Mary Magdalene sees and recognizes Jesus and is told not to cling to him. Matthew's women also see Jesus, cling to his feet, and worship him. It is difficult to harmonize the resurrection accounts, which are full of contradictions in those passages involving women. Luke's version is at the heart of the synoptic story presented here. John's narrative is part of the lectionary reading for Mary Magdalene (p. 157).

◇ **Lectionary Reading**

Jesus journeyed
through cities and villages,

preaching the good news
of the reign of God.
The twelve were with him,
and also women,
many of whom had been healed
of evil spirits and infirmities:
Mary called Magdalene,
from whom seven demons had been expelled,
Joanna, the wife of Chuza, Herod's steward,
and Susanna,
and many others,
who provided for them
out of their personal resources.

◇

Standing by the cross of Jesus
were Mary his mother,
her sister,
Mary the wife of Clopas,
and Mary Magdalene.
There were also women
looking on from afar,
among them,
Mary the mother of James and Joseph,
and Salome the mother of Zebedee's sons,
who, with Mary Magdalene,
followed Jesus
and ministered to him
when he was in Galilee,
and along with many other women,
came up with him to Jerusalem.

In the evening
Joseph from Arimathea,
a rich man who was a disciple,
asked Pilate for the body of Jesus.
He wrapped the body in a clean linen shroud
and put it in his own new tomb
embedded in rock.
He rolled a large stone
to the entrance of the tomb
and departed.
Mary Magdalene
and Mary the mother of Joseph
saw where he was buried,
and they sat

opposite the gravesite
keeping watch.

When the sabbath was over,
Mary Magdalene,
Mary the mother of James,
and Salome,
bought spices to anoint him.
And very early,
on the first day of the week,
they returned to the tomb,
concerned about the large stone
sealing the entrance.
"Who will roll the stone away for us?"
they asked as they were approaching,
but the stone had already been removed.
Entering the tomb
the women saw a white-robed figure seated on the right,
and they were astonished.
"Do not be afraid," the apparition said,
"you seek Jesus who was crucified.
He is not here, he has risen.
Come, see the place where they laid him.
Then go, quickly,
tell the disciples
that he has risen from the dead,
that he is going before you to Galilee,
where you will see him as he said."
They hurried from the tomb
in fear and in joy
and ran to tell the disciples.
It was Mary Magdalene
and Joanna
and Mary the mother of James
and the other women with them
who told this to the apostles,
but their story sounded ridiculous
and they did not believe them.

Later that day
two disciples were returning
to the village of Emmaus,
seven miles from Jerusalem,
discussing everything
that had happened.
As they walked,
they were joined by Jesus,

whom they failed to recognize.
"What are you talking about?" he asked.
The one named Cleopas replied:
"You must be the only one in Jerusalem
who is unaware of all the things
that have happened there these days."
"What things?" he asked.
And they answered,
"Concerning Jesus of Nazareth,
a prophet mighty in word and deed
before God and all the people.
Our religious leaders wanted him dead,
so they had him crucified.
We had hoped that he would be the one
to liberate Israel.
And that is not all.
Today, the third day since he died,
some women of our company
astounded us all.
Early this morning they had gone to the tomb,
but they did not find his body.
They came to us saying
that they had seen a vision of angels
who said that he was alive.
Some who were with us went to the tomb,
and they found it just as the women had described,
but they did not see Jesus."
Then Jesus said,
"O foolish ones!
So slow to believe
all that the prophets have spoken!"

◇ **Personal Reflection**

Word
made flesh,
a recurring
event,
again
and again
God
giving
consent
to an act
of creation,
to life's
liberation

within
every culture
all over the earth.
Wherever
love lives,
it is God
giving birth.

◇ **Points for Shared Reflection**

- Why do you think the authors of the Gospels preserved such conflicting accounts of women's involvement in the resurrection?

- Women remained with the dying Jesus and believed in his resurrection. Reflect on this in contrast to how the twelve male apostles behaved.

- Women accompanied Jesus and the twelve and were among his core of disciples. Luke implies that their contribution was financial support. Who were these women and what do you think their role(s) might have been? In what ways do you accompany Jesus today?

- Luke has been accused of presenting women in a negative light, as either sick, or demented, or promiscuous, or possessed, or otherwise impaired. Is this criticism fair? In what ways does Luke appear to have been both for and against women? How are men today for and against women?

◇ **A Psalm of Discipleship** (see p. 154)

◇ **Prayer**

You call us into discipleship,
O One Who Bears All Burdens,
making a way through the wilderness,
hovering near in pillar and cloud,
revealing bits of Your glory
when all seems hopeless
and courage fails.
Carry us on the wingtips of Your
never-failing promise,
through moments of discouragement
as we push against the tide.
You are my friends,
You told us all,
my friends and my disciples.
Be with us always,
be with us now
as we seek Your way.
Amen.

———— ◇ ————

◇ A PSALM OF DISCIPLESHIP ◇

Choir 1   Bless these hands that reach out
and into the lives
of so many people,
pausing to touch
with tenderness
the hardened heart
where hurt is buried far
beyond all feeling,
where love is a four-letter word
that has no meaning
beyond the now.

Choir 2   Bless these feet that run
through the day
after day
after day
without ceasing,
standing firm
upon principle,
dancing rings around
wanting to quit,
stopping to catch up
with what is important
in the long run,
then and now.

Choir 1   Bless this heart that holds within it
far more than it can carry
of grief
and the disabling
disempowering pain
of multitudes,
yet knows
that You would ask of it
no more than it can bear
and so it bows
in gratitude,
making the most of
amazing grace.

Choir 2   Bless this spirit determined to be
an extension of
Your Spirit,
with a reservoir of compassion
that is conceived
of enough

    By M. T. Winter, Crossroad Pub. Co., © 1990 Medical Mission Sisters

and more than enough
of serenity
and patience
for all Your cherished children,
even if every
replenishing source
but You
were running dry.

Choir 1   We are Your disciples, Shaddai,
may we live for
and love
one another.

Choir 2   Bless our hands to Your service,
our feet to Your path,
our heart to Your purpose,
our spirit
to dwell in the depths
of Your Spirit
for Your glory
now and forever.

By M. T. Winter, Crossroad Pub. Co., © 1990 Medical Mission Sisters

MARY MAGDALENE

◇ **Scripture Reference**　　Luke 8:1–3 / John 19:25; 20:1–18

Mark 15:40–41, 47; 16:1–11
Matthew 27:55–56, 61; 28:1–10
Luke 23:49, 55–56; 24:1–11

◇ **Biography**

It is time to relinquish the false mythology surrounding Mary of Magdala. She was neither prostitute nor penitent, nor was she Luke's public
sinner who washed the feet of Jesus with her tears and wiped them with
her hair, presumptions long supported by Western spirituality and art.
On the other hand, neither is she Mary of Bethany with whom she has
also been confused. She was one of the Galilean women who accompanied Jesus on his mission. Scriptural evidence indicates that she was a
leader in that female circle. Luke suggests that she had been previously

liberated from some serious personal affliction, but whether this was physical or otherwise we will probably never know. We do know that Jesus singled her out for a private revelation on Easter morning, making her the first of all the apostles and disciples to see and proclaim Jesus as risen Christ.

◇ **Context**

Whenever scripture speaks of the Galilean women who followed Jesus, Mary Magdalene heads the list. She is often named with several others, indicating an inner circle of prominence similar to the apostolic leadership of Peter, James, and John. Tradition supports her leadership role, both in the New Testament and in Gnostic writings. In several Gnostic gospels she is portrayed as the spiritual companion of Jesus who alone understood the mysteries of his message and who interpreted these to the others, including the male apostles, some of whom resented her status and the special love Jesus had for her. One can only wonder if the strength of this latter tradition was in some way the basis for discrediting Mary and her historicity. The Gospels give conflicting accounts regarding her presence during major events in the life of Jesus. There is a difference of opinion about whether Mary Magdalene was standing at the foot of the cross as Jesus was dying (John places her there) or watching from a distance. John's account of her experiences on Easter morning differs in certain details from the others, but this can be attributed to the writer's particular theological emphases.

◇ **Lectionary Reading**

Jesus journeyed
through cities and villages,
preaching the good news
of the reign of God.
The twelve were with him,
and also women,
many of whom had been healed
of evil spirits
and infirmities:
Mary called Magdalene,
from whom seven demons had been expelled,
Joanna, the wife of Chuza, Herod's steward,
and Susanna,
and many others,
who provided for them
out of their personal resources.

◇

Standing by the cross of Jesus
were Mary his mother,
her sister,
Mary the wife of Clopas,
and Mary Magdalene.

◇

Mary Magdalene
and Mary the mother of Joseph
saw where he was buried,
and they sat
opposite the gravesite
keeping watch.

◇

Very early
on the first day of the week,
while it was still dark,
Mary Magdalene came to the tomb.
Seeing that the stone had been rolled away,
she ran to Peter and the other disciple,
the one whom Jesus loved, crying,
"They have taken the Master
from the tomb;
we don't know where
they have laid him."
Both men ran,
but the other disciple
reached the tomb before Peter.
Looking in
he saw the linen cloths,
but he hesitated to enter.
Peter arrived
and went into the tomb.
He saw the cloths,
and noticed the head cloth
rolled up and set aside.
The other disciple
also went in,
and he saw,
and he believed.
Until now
they had not understood from scripture
that he would rise again.
Then they left and went back home.

But Mary stood weeping
outside the tomb,
and as she wept
she looked into the tomb
and saw two angels,
all in white,
sitting where the body of Jesus had lain,
one at the head
and one at the feet.
"Why are you weeping?"
they asked her.
"Because they have taken my Master away,
and I do not know where to find him."
Having said this, she turned,
and there was Jesus,
but she did not recognize him.
Then Jesus asked her,
"Why are you weeping?
Whom do you seek?"
Thinking he was the gardener,
she said,
"Sir, if you have removed him,
tell me where you have laid him,
and I will take him away."
Then Jesus whispered,
"Mary."
And Mary shouted,
"Rabboni!"
Eventually, Jesus spoke again.
"You must let me go,
for I must ascend;
but go now and tell the others
that I am returning
to your God and Mine."
So Mary Magdalene
went to the disciples.
"I have seen the Lord!"
she told them.
Then she shared with them
many of the things
that he had said to her.

O Word,
power,
nurturing space,
unspeakable
splendor,
visible trace
of love
loving us
face
to face.
Cult
of all culture
in Whom
we place
our ultimate
yearning,
divine
discerning
turning point
Thou,
flesh of our
flesh
now,
showing us all
how
claim to powers
of transforming
heartwarming
grace
is ours.

◇ **Points for Shared Reflection**

• What happened to Mary Magdalene after the Resurrection? Why do you suppose there is no mention of her in the post-Resurrection church?

• If Mary Magdalene was indeed an apostle to the apostles and first eye-witness to the risen Christ, how could the post-Resurrection church have excluded her from a leadership role? Do you think she was excluded? If not, on what do you base your claims?

• What do you think were the "seven demons" from which she had been released, and how might her past have prepared her for her unique role?

• Do you think Mary Magdalene was at the Last Supper?
If so, how would she have interpreted that event?

• Compare Mary Magdalene's experiences with those of women in ministry today.

- In what ways can Mary Magdalene serve as a role model for women? In what ways might she be a role model for you?

◇ **A Psalm for Women in Leadership** (see p. 162)

◇ **Prayer**

Cling to me
in my hour of need,
O Promised Resurrection.
Reveal to me the power of
Your undefeated love.
Break the bonds that imprison me
in my faults,
fears,
and frustrations.
Let me rise above
patriarchal restraints
to set my sisters free.
O Risen Christa,
proclaim Your truth
now and forever.
Amen.

———— ◇ ————

◇ A PSALM FOR WOMEN IN LEADERSHIP ◇

Choir 1   You lift me up, Shaddai, beyond
my wildest aspirations;
You entrust me with Your mission,
You reveal Your way to me.

Choir 2   In You I pause in the frenzied pace
to gather the lost about me,
to listen to a child's heart break,
to set the imprisoned free.

Choir 1   You give to me, a pauper, gifts
denied the rich and famous;
I live, out of my poverty,
as though possessing all.

Choir 2   In You I take initiative
to rock the staid foundations,
leaving no stone upon a stone
to any dividing wall.

Choir 1   Where is the rule equipped to restrain
the keeper of the vision,
the stone to seal a sepulchre
whose walls are blown away.

Choir 2   Be with me then when men attempt
to render me
defenseless,
when even women
turn from women
compelled to have their say.

Choir 1   The last, the least, the lowest,
these are signs
of Your new creation;
such foolishness is wisdom
that releases
and unlocks.

Choir 2   Now I in You and You in me
make love
make life
make meaning
out of all the sacred subtleties
of Your graced
paradox.

     By M. T. Winter, Crossroad Pub. Co., © 1990 Medical Mission Sisters

MARY, WIFE OF CLEOPAS

◇ **Scripture Reference**   John 19:25
                           Luke 24:13–53

◇ **Biography**

This may well be the most elusive of the many New Testament Marys. Some scholars say that Clopas, the husband of the woman who stood at the foot of the cross, and Cleopas, the disciple on the road to Emmaus, were one and the same. Most do not agree to this association. The Greek text of the Emmaus narrative opens up the possibility that one of the "two of them" leaving Jerusalem might have been a woman. Perhaps Mary was the unnamed disciple accompanying her husband Cleopas back to Emmaus, the one who prepared the meal for the stranger whom they invited into their home. She probably was the woman who stood at the foot of the cross. She certainly was one of the women disciples, but if we agree that she was an Emmaus disciple, then we can conclude that she did not go with Mary Magdalene and the other women to the tomb on Easter morning.

◇ **Context**

Who was the woman at the foot of the cross? Some say Mary the wife of Clopas was Mary the mother of James and Joseph, supposedly the wife of Alphaeus who figured prominently in the Passion narratives. Or could she have been the wife of Cleopas? Scholars point out that there is no linguistic relationship between the Greek name "Cleopas" and the seemingly Semitic "Clopas," but grammarians say the interchanging of the names may have been a common occurrence.

While the names present a problem, the critical question concerns the gender of the two on the road to Emmaus. Contrary to a long tradition of homiletic assumptions, the Greek reference to "two of them" (*duo es auton*) implies no specific gender. Although other pronouns in the text favor the interpretation that both disciples were men, some commentators support the possibility that the second traveller was the wife of Cleopas. The suggestion that the "two of them" did include a woman is strengthened by the reference to "some women of our company" in verse 22, literally "some women of us" (one is tempted to say, "some of us women"). It seems more appropriate for a woman to be telling about what these women had seen, since the men did not believe them.

The Emmaus episode is Luke's redaction, perhaps even creative reconstruction, of a pre-existing tradition (see Mk 16:12–13) and contains traditional embellishments as well as Luke's particular theological emphases. It is the second of four resurrection narratives recorded in chapter 24. In the first the women find an empty tomb, but do not see the risen Jesus. At the close of the Emmaus narrative, Christ appears to Simon (Peter), so it is said, although there are no details, and then appears to all the apostles and those disciples who were together with them. In contrast to the other three Gospel writers, Luke does not attribute the first revelation and proclamation of the risen Christ to women. Might Luke also have excluded the woman from the event's first interpretation? Perhaps the eucharistic implications of the Emmaus episode were too significant. For if a woman were to have recognized Jesus in the way he blessed and broke the bread, wouldn't women insist that she was also present at the Last Supper?

The Emmaus story requires interpretation, and Christianity has long lacked female interpreters. If we accept the wife of Cleopas as one of the Emmaus disciples, then according to Luke she and her husband were also present at the remaining events of chapter 24. Because Luke alone excludes women from their established position as historical eyewitnesses to the resurrected Christ and implies that Jesus appeared first to Peter, we can assume that there is more to the early tradition concerning women than is evident from the texts.

Standing by the cross of Jesus
were Mary his mother,
her sister,
Mary the wife of Clopas,
and Mary Magdalene.

◇

Later that day
two disciples were returning
to the village of Emmaus,
seven miles from Jerusalem,
discussing everything
that had happened.
As they walked,
they were joined by Jesus,
whom they failed to recognize.
"What are you talking about?" he asked.
The one named Cleopas replied:
"You must be the only one in Jerusalem
who is unaware of all the things
that have happened there these days."
"What things?" he asked.
And they answered,
"Concerning Jesus of Nazareth,
a prophet mighty in word and deed
before God and all the people.
Our religious leaders wanted him dead,
so they had him crucified.
We had hoped that he would be the one
to liberate Israel.
And that is not all.
Today, the third day since he died,
some women of our company
astounded us all.
Early this morning
they had gone to the tomb,
but they did not find his body.
They came to us saying
that they had seen a vision of angels
who said that he was alive.
Some who were with us
went to the tomb,
and they found it just as the women had described,
but they did not see Jesus."
Then Jesus said,

"O foolish ones!
So slow to believe
all that the prophets have spoken!
Was it not ordained
that the Christ should suffer
and so enter into his glory?"
Then beginning with Moses
and mentioning all the prophets,
he explained to them
those passages in scripture
referring to himself.

As they approached the village
to which they were heading,
he appeared to be going further,
but they begged him to remain with them.
"Stay with us,
evening is coming
and the day is nearly over."
So he went in to stay with them.
Now while he was with them at table,
he took the bread
and said the blessing,
then broke it
and gave it to them.
Their eyes were opened
and they recognized him,
but he had vanished from their sight.
Then they said to each other,
"Were our hearts not burning within us
when he talked to us on the road
and explained the scriptures to us?"
They went out at once
and returned to Jerusalem.
There they found the eleven
gathered with those
who were with them,
who said:
"Yes, it is true.
Jesus has risen
and has appeared to Simon."
Then they told their story
of what happened on the road
and how they recognized him
in the breaking of the bread.

As they were speaking,

Jesus stood among them
and said:
"Peace be with you!"
They were startled
and frightened
and thought it was a ghost.
"Why are you so agitated,"
he asked them,
"and why do these doubts
arise in your hearts?
Look at my hands and my feet;
touch me and see for yourselves,
it is I.
A ghost has no flesh or bones
as I have."
Their joy was so great,
they just could not believe it,
so he said to them,
"Have you anything here to eat?"
They gave him a piece of grilled fish,
and they stood there and watched
as he ate it.

Then he said to them:
"This is what I meant
when I said to you
while I was still among you,
that everything written about me
in the law of Moses
and in the Prophets
and in the Psalms
had to be fulfilled."
Then he opened their minds
to understand the scriptures,
and he said to them,
"So you see how it is written
that the Christ should suffer
and on the third day
rise from the dead,
and that repentance
and the forgiveness of sins
would be preached
in his name
to all nations,
beginning in Jerusalem.
You are witnesses to this.

And now I will send the promise
of God our Creator
upon you.
Stay in the city
until you are clothed with the power
from on high."

Then he took them with him
to the outskirts of Bethany,
and lifting up his hands
he blessed them,
and as he blessed them,
he withdrew from them
and was carried up into heaven.
They returned to Jerusalem
full of joy,
and were continually in the temple
praising God.

◇ **Personal Reflection**

Star night
alone
bone weary
wary
a word
a chord
might penetrate
the thin façade
spilling the pain
inadvertently,
when kindness
another name for God
took time
simply to be
with me
and I could begin
living again
from the inside
out
instead of the outside
in.

◇ **Points for Shared Reflection**

- Reflect on the Emmaus story as though the two disciples were husband
  and wife. How does this interpretation feel to you? Is it consistent with
  the main story line of the text?

- Go back to the traditional interpretation and imagine two men on the road to Emmaus. Is this still an acceptable alternative for you? If so, why? If not, why not?
- Understanding did not come to the disciples through the convincing arguments of theological interpretation but through an intuitive flash during a shared experience in a moment of ritual. How does insight usually come to you? How have you experienced the power of ritual?
- Why would Luke preserve a different set of facts concerning eyewitnesses to the risen Jesus, excluding women and recording instead an appearance of Christ to Peter?
- Do you think women were present at the Last Supper? Who do you think was there, and why?

◇ **An Easter Psalm** (see p. 170)

◇ **Prayer**
We praise You, O Resurrected Hope,
for exceeding our expectations,
for breaking to bits
the narrow scope
of our finite comprehension.
Who could have guessed
You would walk with us
on our journey into meaning,
instead of sending us
out on our own
to find the promised land.
May we never lose sight
of that empty tomb
that symbolizes resurrection,
never forget
that only the dead
are capable of rising.
Take the bread of our
limited experience
and break it to our advantage,
revealing a vision
of healing and hope
for all who come home
to God.
For this we pray,
this day and always.
Amen.

———— ◇ ————

⬦ AN EASTER PSALM ⬦

Choir 1   Hail, O Resurrected Hope,
spilling over
the hills of our grief
like the blush of a new day
dawning.

Choir 2   Hail, Sudden Sabbath Surprise,
spark of fire
in our verbal ash,
cognitive flash
like the fleeting glimmer
of recognition
in a newborn baby's
eyes.

Choir 1   The Word is risen,
the miracle continues,
say amen, alleluia!

Choir 2   The Song is risen,
the music continues,
sing amen, alleluia!

Choir 1   Happy the feet that dance
the Good News
in the civilized streets
of the nations.

Choir 2   Happy the heart that hears
and tells
of Easter
at all the village wells,
country pumps,
steel cells,
ghetto dumps,
where so much of life
lies buried.

Choir 1   Praise the One Who is raised
to life,
let the trumpets
break their silence
in articulated
creeds.

By M. T. Winter, Crossroad Pub. Co., © 1990 Medical Mission Sisters

Choir 2   Praise the One Who raises
to life
a community
of believers
with a fanfare
of impossible deeds.

Choir 1   Christ is the One Who gives wings
to our freedom,
lifting
our inner selves
higher
than wild birds borne
by the will
of the wind.

Choir 2   Christ is the free fall
of faith
unencumbered
by guidelines
or more guarantees.

Choir 1   Hail, O One Who is warm to our touch,
neither death
nor doubt
can contain You.

Choir 2   Hail, O One Who eludes our touch,
only by faith
can we know You.

By M. T. Winter, Crossroad Pub. Co., © 1990 Medical Mission Sisters   *WomanWord* / **171**

◇ III ◇
Women and the Spirit
of Jesus
and Shaddai

WOMEN AT PENTECOST

◇ **Scripture Reference**   Acts 1:12–14 / Acts 2:1–18

◇ **Biography**

Without a doubt there were women in the upper room at Pentecost, women who were present when the Holy Spirit appeared in the form of tongues of fire. Mary the mother of Jesus was there along with family members. So were other women, as indicated in the Book of Acts. While they are not named as are the apostles, surely numbered among those present were Mary Magdalene and others who had accompanied Jesus during his life, who stood by him while he was dying, and who went to the tomb on Easter morning. Strangers in the streets of Jerusalem heard women as well as men tell of the wonderful works of God.

The presence of women at Pentecost has been overshadowed in an effort to show that men have always played a central role in the church. Liturgical tradition has focused its Pentecost celebrations on chapter 2 of Acts, which begins: "When the day of Pentecost had come, they were all together in one place. . . . " It has been left to preachers and teachers and interpreters to tell us who "they" were, and only recently have any of these bothered to turn back to chapter 1 with its notation about the women (vs. 14). The natural linkage of this verse to the beginning of chapter 2 is broken by the election of Matthias to replace Judas the betrayer, clearly an interpolation which serves to separate the sections. Liturgical art has not helped the cause of women with its images of twelve bearded men beneath twelve tongues of flame. Male oriented translations have supported this biased interpretation. However, women were present at Pentecost, and consequently women also were empowered by the Holy Spirit to preach and to testify. That was the point of the passage from Joel which Peter used to explain and, yes, to justify what must have appeared as utter chaos, women in the streets of Jerusalem enthusiastically proclaiming the praises of God.

◇ **Lectionary Reading**

They returned to Jerusalem
from the Mount of Olives,
a sabbath day's walk from the city,
and entered the upper room
where they were staying,
Peter and John and James and Andrew,
Philip and Thomas,
Bartholomew and Matthew,
James, the son of Alphaeus,
Simon the Zealot,
and Jude, the son of James.
With one heart
they devoted themselves to prayer,
together with the women,
and Mary the mother of Jesus,
and his brothers
and his sisters.

When the day of Pentecost came around,
they were all together there
in that room,
when suddenly the sound
of a rushing wind
shook the house
where they were sitting,

and they saw
what seemed like
tongues of fire
hovering above
each one of them,
and all were filled
with the Holy Spirit
and began to speak
in different tongues
in the power of the Spirit.
Hearing this sound,
a crowd assembled,
devout people
from every nation known on earth,
Parthians, Medes, and Elamites,
people from Mesopotamia,
from Judea and Cappadocia,
Pontus and Asia,
Phrygia and Pamphylia,
Egypt and the parts of Libya around Cyrene,
Jews and proselytes,
Cretans and Arabians
who were visiting from Rome.
All were amazed and astonished,
for all of them heard
their own language,
heard them preach
in their own language
the wonderful works of God.
They tried to laugh it off, saying:
"They drank too much new wine."
But Peter stood up
and, raising his voice,
contradicted them.
"We are not drunk
as you suppose.
It is only the beginning
of the day.
These words of the prophet
have come to pass:

'In the days to come,
it is God Who speaks,
I will pour out My Spirit
on all humankind.
Your daughters and sons

shall prophesy.
The young shall see visions.
The old shall dream dreams.
Even on My slaves,
both women and men,
I will pour out My Spirit
in those days,
and they shall prophesy.' "

◇ **Personal Reflection**

Holy Spirited
spirits
speak of mysteries
in whispers
among the grasses,
incantations
in the trees,
resurrect
forgotten formulas,
antiphonal
responses
to long lost
litanies,
concealing
their *axis mundi*
and transient
deities.
Tell me,
O Holy of Holies,
can Your
creative
power
circumvent
canonicity
to communicate
through
such as these?

◇ **Points for Shared Reflection**

- Who do you suppose was in that upper room when the day of Pentecost arrived?

- On the basis of chapter 2 of Acts, what ought to be the church's position with regard to male and female participation in the life of the church?

- It has been said that the Spirit is the feminine or female principle in the Deity. Do you agree? Can you as a woman relate to God more easily through the Spirit?

- What dream do you dream for yourself as a woman who is loved by God and in whom God's Spirit dwells?
- What dream do you dream for the world which God's own Spirit called into being back in the beginning?
- What kind of future do you envision for the church globally, nationally, locally?

◇ **A Pentecost Psalm** (see p. 179)

◇ **Prayer**
  O Spirit of God
  and God of the spirit,
  O Principle of Grace
  who fashions us
  in the image of Shaddai,
  we cry out to You
  for a new beginning,
  a new age pentecost
  that will truly shake us,
  break us, remake us
  in the image of Your *Koinonia*,
  where all are one
  in one another,
  loving and loved
  by You,
  now and forever.
  Amen.

———— ◇ ————

◊ A PENTECOST PSALM ◊

Choir 1 Praise to You, O Primeval Fire,
filling
the belly of earth
and of us
with the flame of
infinity,
transforming us
as You burn within us,
build within us
an all-consuming
love.

Choir 2 Praise to You, Eternal Flame,
dawn,
high noon
of our soul's
awareness,
light in the night
when the child in us
cries,
starlight
dancing
in love's
loving eyes.

Choir 1 Voice of the Word
made world,
Genesis
of all life,
all love
in the beginning,
hovering over
the chaos
until it willed
its own creation,
recreate us
in the midst
of all the mistakes
of our own making.

Choir 2 O Essence of All Inspiration,
breathe new meaning
and purpose
into our dull
dispirited
species,

give us a vision
of Your new creation,
be dream,
insight,
intuition
and a second sense
susceptible
to discerning Your ways
within us.

Choir 1   O Singer of All Sacred Song,
make melody in us
and through us
until our hearts beat
to the rhythms rehearsed
in our soul-shaping
solitudes,
until heart
unto heart
heralds those notes
composed in the key
of compassion,
until the whole world
vibrates as one
with the shared harmonic
of hope.

Choir 2   O Music of the Eternal Spheres,
You touch our hearts
like harps
and hear the clear tones
of Your lovesong,
You blow through our souls
like wind in a flute
in a rippling rush
of peace.

Choir 1   O Giver of Gifts,
give us the gift
of ourselves,
and the gift
of a genuine
self surrender
to the how
of our heart's maturing
and the who
of our becoming

        By M. T. Winter, Crossroad Pub. Co., © 1990 Medical Mission Sisters

and the why
of our believing

Choir 2   O Gift of the Giver,
pour out upon us
Your power
and promise,
and be in us
gift
for one another
as we give each other
You.

Choir 1   We praise You,
O One Who Holds and Heals
broken body
and broken spirit,
be wholeness
in us
and wholly
within us,
visible inside
and out.

Choir 2   We praise You, Whom we know
yet do not know,
may we always
sing Your praises,
empowered by Your spirit
poured out anew
in a never-ending
pentecost.

By M. T. Winter, Crossroad Pub. Co., © 1990 Medical Mission Sisters

SAPPHIRA

◇ **Scripture Reference**   Acts 5:1–11

◇ **Biography**

Sapphira and her husband Ananias were members of the primitive church in Jerusalem where all things were said to be held in common. Both were struck dead on the spot after lying to Peter about the amount of money they had received from the sale of a piece of property.

◇ **Context**

This story may have been meant to function as a midrash or legend that is told to make a point. The narrative preceding it tells of a man who sold his field and gave all the proceeds to the church. Sapphira's story relates a similar transaction, only some of the profits are withheld. The consequences of hypocrisy are divine retribution which is swift and unequivocal. Stories such as these are tools for teaching. This may well have been part of a homily, as the church is obviously in session from certain clues within the text. The point of the story is that one is free to choose or not to choose to commit oneself completely, but one's choice must be rooted in truth. There are no doubt many other points, such as equity and equality. Since material possessions were a sign of God's blessing, it would take some hard lessons for Jewish Christians to learn about the value of *koinonia* and poverty.

The implications of gender equality are that women and men share equally in the consequences of their shared decisions. However, God's response, death without mercy, contradicts the spirit of Jesus who preaches forgiveness and a second chance. The term "church" appears here for the first time in Acts and means both the whole body of believers and the local congregation. If the story is indeed homiletic narrative, does this mean that Sapphira is not a historical figure? Not necessarily. Most stories contain a basis of truth. A similar incident may well have happened and been embellished over time. In the absence of evidence to the contrary, we presume this to be so.

◇ **Lectionary Reading**

There was a man, Ananias,
who with his wife Sapphira's knowledge
sold a piece of property
and held on to some of the money.
The rest of the proceeds from the sale
they presented to the apostles.
"Ananias," Peter said,
"how has Satan so possessed you
that you should lie to the Holy Spirit
about keeping some of the money
you received from this sale?
Before the land was sold,
wasn't it yours?
And after you sold it,
wasn't the money also yours
to dispose of as you wished?
What led you to this deception?
You have lied, not to people,
but to God."
When Ananias heard these words,
he dropped dead on the spot.
Now all this
made a profound impression
on everyone who was present.
Several young men came forward,
covered him up,
carried him out
and buried him.
About three hours later
his wife came in,
unaware of what had happened.
Peter challenged her.
"Tell me, is this the amount of money
you received for the sale of your land?"

"Yes," she said, "it is."
Then Peter said,
"You and your husband have conspired together
to test the Spirit of God.
What made you do such a thing?
Do you hear those footsteps?
The feet of those who buried your husband
are coming now for you."
And she dropped dead at his feet.
The young men came
and carried her out
and buried her
beside her husband.
Now all this
made a profound impression
on the whole church
and on all who heard it.

◇ **Personal Reflection**

Something
sacred
this day
comes,
spread the Word
through
the talking drums.
King of the jungle,
Prince of the plain,
Lord of lands
where saints
were slain,
Milk of compassion,
nurturing Rain,
please
come as a woman
when you come
again.

◇ **Points for Shared Reflection**

• Reflect on some of the points of this story as discussed in the commentary under "Context." What other points came to mind as you listened to the reading?

• If the narrative is in fact an embellishment of an earlier event, is it possible that Sapphira was originally an innocent victim of her husband's greed and duplicity? What would be the reasons for recasting the incident in its present form?

- What are some lessons you have learned from Sapphira's story that can be applied to your own life?

- The story suggests that Sapphira had two images, the public and the private. Can this be said of you? What are some ways of integrating what we say with what we do?

◇ **A Psalm of Desire for Truth** (see p. 186)

◇ **Prayer**

True to all who call upon You
are You, true God, true Goodness.
We who are made in Your image
long to be genuine images
of all that You truly are,
not superficial copies
that walk and talk like gods.
Speak truth through us clearly
so that all who hear will know
we belong to You,
are one with You,
in Spirit and truth.
Amen.

——— ◇ ———

◇ A PSALM OF DESIRE FOR TRUTH ◇

Choir 1   To You we call, True God and Savior,
in Whom there is no prevarication,
no lies, no duplicity.

Choir 2   Make of us, here and now, true believers,
who walk the ways of integrity
and live lives that are true.

Choir 1   So much of our world is artificial,
superficial,
counterfeit or fake,
parading its false premises,
hawking its imitations,
pretending it is genuine.

Choir 2   So many around us live the lie
and are trapped
in its innuendos.
So what is truth? they ask,
out of their bold hypocrisies,
remaining immune
to what is authentic.

Choir 1   Give me an honest heart, O God;
help me to say
what I want to say,
what I ought to say,
unconcerned about pleasing people
or being easy
on myself.

Choir 2   Give me a truth-telling tongue, O God,
that will not hesitate
to call the question,
no matter what the consequences,
the circumstance,
the risk.

Choir 1   You are the Way, the Truth,
the Life that is lived
wholly transparent:
give us transparency.

Choir 2   Your Word Who is truth says,
keep my word,
speak the truth,
and the truth will make you free
and keep you true
to Me.

 By M. T. Winter, Crossroad Pub. Co., © 1990 Medical Mission Sisters

DORCAS (TABITHA)

◇ **Scripture Reference**   Acts 9:36–42

◇ **Biography**

Dorcas, called a disciple, was loved and revered among the widows of Jaffa, a Mediterranean port city to the north of Jerusalem. Widely praised for her talented sewing and many charitable works, she died after an illness and was raised to life again by Peter. The name Dorcas is Greek — the Aramaic is Tabitha.

◇ **Context**

The only person to be raised from the dead by an apostle was a woman, Dorcas, and many became believers because of this miracle. Peter's actions call to mind Jesus' raising of Jairus's daughter, which he had witnessed. The word "disciple" used to identify Dorcas is the only occurrence of the feminine form of that word in the entire New Testament. In this context, "disciple" seems to describe those with authority.

◇ **Lectionary Reading**

Now at Jaffa there was a disciple
whose name was Tabitha,
in Greek it is Dorcas,
who was tireless in doing good

187

and in charitable giving.
She fell ill and died,
and they prepared her body
and laid her in an upper room.
Now Peter was nearby in Lydda,
and when the disciples heard
he was in that town,
they sent two men with an urgent message,
to come as soon as possible.
So Peter went back with them at once,
and when he arrived,
they took him to the upper room
where all the widows were gathered in tears,
displaying the tunics and other garments
Dorcas had made when she was with them.
Peter sent all of them out of the room.
Then he knelt, and prayed,
and turning to the body, he said,
"Tabitha, get up."
She opened her eyes, looked at Peter, and sat up.
Peter gave her his hand, and she stood up.
Then he called in the saints and widows
and he presented her to them, alive.
The whole of Jaffa heard the news,
and many became believers.

◇ **Personal Reflection**

Wind in the pines
on a moonlight
night
makes
the whole of me
homesick
for
the woods
of my childhood
summers
when
alone
on a stone
fence
I would hear
the breakers
on the eternal
shore,
making me ache

then
and now
even more
for being
drawn
into Being.
So young
was I
to fantasize
that wind
in the pines
is when God
sighs
for all grace fails
to realize
in me,
no matter
how intense
the mystical
experience.

◇ **Points for Shared Reflection**

- What symbolic connections can you see between the upper room in Jerusalem and the one in Jaffa, particularly regarding women?

- To raise someone from the dead is an act of some significance and a not-too-common occurrence. Why is it that the story of Dorcas is so unfamiliar to most Christians?

- Reflect some more on Dorcas. What does your intuition tell you of her? What might have been her role in the church and in her community?

◇ **A Psalm of Women Rising** (see p. 190)

◇ **Prayer**

Rise up, O God of Death-to-Life,
and carry us all with You
from the tomb of our affliction
into Your brand new day,
where there is no more
keeping down or holding back
or passing over any person,
no more discrimination,
but in the fullness of Your justice,
all are equal, women and men,
and all are one in You. Amen.

———— ◇ ————

◇ A PSALM OF WOMEN RISING ◇

Chorus Here and there, women are rising,
everywhere, women are rising, rising from the dead.

All Here and there, women are rising,
everywhere, women are rising, rising from the dead.

Chorus	From their silence . . .	*All*	Women are rising!
Chorus	From their bondage . . .	*All*	Women are rising!
Chorus	From exclusion . . .	*All*	Women are rising!
Chorus	From exploitation . . .	*All*	Women are rising!
Chorus	From rape and incest . . .	*All*	Women are rising!
Chorus	From their guilt . . .	*All*	Women are rising!
Chorus	From all affliction . . .	*All*	Women are rising!
Chorus	From all addiction . . .	*All*	Women are rising!
Chorus	Against all odds . . .	*All*	Women are rising!

All Here and there, women are rising,
everywhere, women are rising, rising from the dead.

Chorus	Like the sun . . .	*All*	Women are rising!
Chorus	Like the moon . . .	*All*	Women are rising!
Chorus	Like a kite . . .	*All*	Women are rising!
Chorus	Like an eagle . . .	*All*	Women are rising!
Chorus	Like the tide . . .	*All*	Women are rising!
Chorus	Like a prayer . . .	*All*	Women are rising!
Chorus	Just like incense . . .	*All*	Women are rising!
Chorus	Just like bread . . .	*All*	Women are rising!
Chorus	Just like Dorcas . . .	*All*	Women are rising!

All Here and there, women are rising,
everywhere, women are rising, rising from the dead.

Chorus	Into hope . . .	*All*	Women are rising!
Chorus	Into freedom . . .	*All*	Women are rising!
Chorus	Into speech . . .	*All*	Women are rising!
Chorus	Into power . . .	*All*	Women are rising!
Chorus	Into partnership . . .	*All*	Women are rising!
Chorus	Into significance . . .	*All*	Women are rising!
Chorus	Into the future . . .	*All*	Women are rising!

All Here and there, women are rising,
everywhere, women are rising, rising from the dead.

  By M. T. Winter, Crossroad Pub. Co., © 1990 Medical Mission Sisters

RHODA

◇ **Scripture Reference**   Acts 12:11–17

◇ **Biography**

Rhoda was a female servant in the household of Mary the mother of John Mark in Jerusalem. Late one night she heard a persistent knocking. When she discovered it was Peter, she became so flustered, she left him standing at the gate.

◇ **Context**

Herod's soldiers had just killed James the brother of John and thrown Peter in prison. He was there under a double guard, awaiting a summons to appear before Herod. In the middle of the night, Peter is miraculously led from prison by a heavenly apparition. He hurries to the home of Mary the mother of John Mark, a meeting place for Christians in Jerusalem. The community, deeply concerned about Peter, is gathered there in prayer.

◇ **Lectionary Reading**

All of a sudden it occurred to Peter:
"God really did send an angel
to deliver me from Herod
and from all that the Jewish people
were so certain would happen to me."
On realizing this,
he went straight to the home of Mary,
John Mark's mother,
where many had gathered in prayer.
He knocked at the courtyard gate
and a maid named Rhoda responded,
who recognized Peter's voice.
In her excitement,
she ran to tell the others
and left him standing at the gate.
"You are mad," they said to her,
but she insisted it was so.
"It is his guardian angel," they replied.
Meanwhile, the knocking continued,
and when they opened the gate and saw him,
they were absolutely amazed.
Peter motioned to them to be silent,
then told them how an angel of God
had rescued him from prison.
"Tell this to James and the others," he said,
then he left for another place.

◇ **Personal Reflection**

Make me
a window,
not a wall,
demolish
defenses,
let barriers
fall.
O Window
of Wisdom,
look
into me
with an eye
to compassion,

forgive
what you see,
and as light
through a prism,
so may I be
reflection
of Your sacred
transparency.

◇ **Points for Shared Reflection**

• The question is, where was James, the brother of Jesus, who was supposedly in charge of the Jerusalem church. Was he hiding out from Herod?
Or did he belong to another worshiping community that was meeting
somewhere else?

• This vignette of Rhoda adds a humorous touch to the early church chron-
icles. In what way is Rhoda like Peter? Do you identify at all with her?

• Once again we read how a female eyewitness relates what she has seen
and heard and nobody believes her. The church does not believe her.
Recall other instances when the church has not believed women in the
past or in the present.

◇ **A Psalm for Women Believers** (see p. 194)

◇ **Prayer**
O God, we believe,
help the unbelief
of a doubting institution
which relies
far more heavily
on its own interpretations
than the priorities
of Your ways.
May women stand firm
in the faith
that is rooted
in their own faith experience,
confident that You
in Spirit and truth
are validation
for us all.
Amen.

———— ◇ ————

◇ A PSALM FOR WOMEN BELIEVERS ◇

Leader   Women witnessed an empty tomb,
    All   but the church did not believe them.

Leader   Mary Magdalene saw the risen Christ,
    All   but the church did not believe her.

Leader   Rhoda saw Peter freed from prison,
    All   but the church did not believe her.

Leader   Joan of Arc heard heaven speak,
    All   but the church did not believe her.

Leader   Female mystics saw visions of God,
    All   but the church did not believe them.

Leader   Anne Hutchinson spoke of the Spirit's indwelling,
    All   but the church did not believe her.

Leader   Mary Dyer preached God's word,
    All   but the church did not believe her.

Leader   Bridget Bishop said she was not a witch,
    All   but the church did not believe her.

Leader   Women have said, we are not slaves,
    All   but the church did not believe them.

Leader   Women have been excommunicated,
    All   because the church did not believe them.

Leader   Women have been condemned as heretics,
    All   because the church did not believe them.

Leader   Women have been burned to death at the stake,
    All   because the church did not believe them.

Leader   Eleven Episcopal women said they were priests,
    All   but the church did not believe them.

Leader   Women said a woman could be bishop,
    All   but the church did not believe them.

Leader   Other women say they are called to be priests,
    All   but the church does not believe them.

Leader   Other women say they are called to preach,
    All   but the church does not believe them.

Leader   Women say God works in womanly ways,
    All   but the church does not believe them.

Leader   Faith means believing
      the unbelievable,
      unpredictable God.
    All   May we never doubt Your word, Shaddai,
      should You choose to speak through us.

MARY, MOTHER OF JOHN MARK

◇ **Scripture Reference**   Acts 12:11–17

◇ **Biography**

It is generally accepted that Mary was host to a house church in Jerusalem. It has been suggested that those who gathered with her were a group of Hellenists who differed from the Jewish Christians that gathered around James. Some feel very strongly that she was in charge of the church that met at her house and that she most likely presided at its Eucharist. She was independently wealthy, had a large home and servants, and was the mother of John Mark who was a cousin to Barnabas (Col 4:10). She may also have been a widow. The fact that scripture records her name attests to her importance in the Jerusalem community, as does the fact that Peter went straight to her place following his escape from prison, where he charged her and those who were gathered there with reporting the news of his safety to James, the head of the Jerusalem church. Mary not only knew Peter personally, but through her son also had access to Paul.

◇ **Context**

There is a tradition that claims Mary's house was the site of the Last Supper, but this probably wasn't true. It is possible, however, that it served as the headquarters of the Jerusalem church. Peter seems to have been there often enough so that even the maid recognizes him simply by the sound of his voice. Many things have been said of Mary's son, John Mark, some facts and a lot of fiction. We know for certain that he went with Paul and Barnabas to Antioch on their first missionary journey, that he abandoned Paul midway and returned to Jerusalem, possibly because of Paul's handling of his cousin Barnabas, that Paul refused to take him on a second journey, choosing instead to go with Silas. Eventually there was a reconciliation between John Mark and Paul. On the other hand, there is nothing to substantiate the suggestion that John Mark is the author of the second Gospel.

◇ **Lectionary Reading**

All of a sudden it occurred to Peter:
"God really did send an angel
to deliver me from Herod
and from all that the Jewish people
were so certain would happen to me."
On realizing this,
he went straight to the home of Mary,
John Mark's mother,
where many had gathered in prayer.
He knocked at the courtyard gate
and a maid named Rhoda responded,
who recognized Peter's voice.
In her excitement,
she ran to tell the others
and left him standing at the gate.
"You are mad," they said to her,
but she insisted it was so.
"It is his guardian angel," they replied.
Meanwhile, the knocking continued,
and when they opened the gate
and saw him,
they were absolutely amazed.
Peter motioned to them to be silent,

then told them how an angel of God
had rescued him from prison.
"Tell this to James and the others," he said,
then he left for another place.

◇ **Personal Reflection**

There is nothing
so dark
as an African night:
no moon
no star
no trace of light
defines the space
we occupy.
When in darkness,
why not try
to replace suggestions
of the eye
with insight
born of solitude;
give wisdom
a chance
to wander by
before distractions
again intrude
and we are forced
once more
to be
beguiled
defiled
by what we see.

◇ **Points for Shared Reflection**

- Imagine you are part of the community that meets in Mary's house. You are present for the Eucharist, and Mary is presiding. Describe the ritual from what you know about the early liturgy of the Jerusalem church (see Acts, chapters 2 and 4).

- Why is it feasible to conclude that Mary was in charge of the church at her house and presided at Eucharist? Give reasons related to facts as well as intuition.

- In what ways does female leadership in today's church resemble that of Mary, mother of John Mark?

◇ **A Psalm for the Gathered Community** (see p. 199)

◇ **Prayer**

O God of grace and eternal good,
You gather us all together
like a parent
with Her children.
You listen to our petitions
and You welcome our words of praise.
There are times when we find no comfort
in theological remembrance,
but simply take
from Your gentle touch
a strength to meet our need.
Be with us now and always
in the community of believers,
and free us from a dependency
on our paraments
of praise.
Amen.

———— ◇ ————

◇ A PSALM FOR THE GATHERED COMMUNITY ◇

Choir 1   Blessed are we who are glad to be part
of the household
of the faith,

Choir 2   who gather to pray
from time to time,
remembering all who are in need
of the strength
of our support.

Choir 1   Blessed are we who love to sing
new songs
of inspiration,

Choir 2   whose hearts are moved
by the rhythms
and the harmonies
of praise.

Choir 1   Blessed are we when the bread
we break
corresponds to our cry
for justice,

Choir 2   when the cup we take
reiterates
those covenants sealed
in blood.

Choir 1   Blessed are we when the word proclaims
our own love's
liberation,

Choir 2   freedom from fascination
with the lure
of transient gods.

Choir 1   Blessed are You, O Welcoming One,
Who lifts the yoke
of our bondage,

Choir 2   and blessed are we who shelter within
the shade
of Your outstretched wing.

LYDIA

◇ **Scripture Reference**   Acts 16:11–15, 40

◇ **Biography**

Lydia was a business woman who came from Thyatira, a city in Lydia in
Asia Minor. Her name, therefore, may originally have been a descriptive
adjective denoting her homeland. She was a seller of dyed goods for
which her city of origin was famous. She herself traded specifically in
purple goods, a luxury item, indicating she was financially well off and
influential. She had a home in Philippi and worshiped with a circle
of Jewish women, although she herself was probably not a Jew. The
term "God-fearer" meant a Gentile who attended Jewish services and
accepted basic Jewish teachings about the one true God. After hearing
Paul who addressed the women at one of their sabbath services, she was
converted, and eventually she was baptized along with the members of

her household. Paul accepted her invitation to stay in her home, to which he returned after his release from prison. Lydia was a major figure in the apostolic church. The church at Philippi began with her conversion and she may well have led the house church which met in her home.

◇ **Context**

The major overland route from Asia to the West passed through the city of Philippi in Macedonia, making it an ideal location for merchants and traders. Lydia was well situated for her role in the emerging church and must have been a woman of considerable wealth. She seems to have provided both hospitality and financial support to Paul, an exception to his personal policy of working for his living. The group of Christian believers that met at her house were most likely a church. House churches were vital to the missionary movement, for they provided a meeting place and leadership for liturgies of the Word and of the Eucharist. After Paul's release from prison, where he had been placed after he exorcised a female slave supposedly possessed by a demon (see p. 206), he returned to Lydia's house to encourage the community gathered there. Paul's letter to the church at Philippi is indicative of his unique love for the Philippian Christians. Surely Lydia was directly responsible for many of the positive experiences to which he refers.

◇ **Lectionary Reading**

We set out from Troas
and sailed directly to Samothrace,
and on the next day,
to Neapolis,
and from there to Philippi,
a Roman colony and a significant city
of Macedonia.
After we had been there for several days,
we went to a customary place of prayer
outside the gates and along the river,
because it was the sabbath,
and we preached to the women
who had gathered there.
One of these, named Lydia,
a devout woman from Thyatira
who was a seller of dyed purple goods,
listened closely to Paul.
God touched her heart to accept what she heard,
and eventually she was baptized,
along with her household.
She then sent an invitation to Paul, saying,
"If you really accept me as a true believer,

come and stay with us in our house."
And she would not take no for an answer.

◇

From prison Paul and Silas
returned to Lydia's house
where they saw the community of believers,
and they encouraged them,
and then they left.

◇ **Personal Reflection**

Salt
of the earth
is the salt
of the sea,
psalter
of integral
lived
liturgy,
savor
the strength
of it,
embrace
the length
of its surf
slowly
surfacing,
savoring
me.

◇ **Points for Shared Reflection**

- The leadership qualities necessary to make it in the business world may have served to make Lydia a leader in the Philippian church as well. Try to reconstruct the missing lines of her story from this point of view.

- There is no indication that Lydia left her profession after her conversion. Wealth and status seem compatible with following Jesus in the emerging church. Compare this with the Gospel perspective. Can you defend a ministry of money in the church? If so, according to what criteria?

- As a woman in the workplace, or one involved in a business or profession outside the home, comment on the challenge of being a good Christian in professional or commercial settings.

- Name some ways of achieving a closer integration between ministry in the church and ministry in the wider world. Have you been able to achieve such an integration? If not, why not?

◇ **A Psalm for Working Women** (see p. 204)

◇ **Prayer**

Worker Woman God,
we thank You and we praise You
for Your images of labor,
those metaphors of meaning
that give substance to our lives of toil
and bond us closer to You.
Surely the one who wrote Your story
lacks some understanding,
for females in Your image
seldom rest
their seventh day.
Be with us
in our hectic pace,
be the still place
deep within us,
and give to us
sweet sabbath rest
when our work day
is done.
Amen.

——— ◇ ———

◇ A PSALM FOR WORKING WOMEN ◇

All   Six days You worked, Wonder Worker God,
and on the seventh day You rested.

Choir 1   Six days to fashion a universe and a world
of Your own making,
meticulously calling forth
land and sky
independently
from the waters.

All   Six days You worked, Wonder Worker God,
and on the seventh day You rested.

Choir 2   Six days to fasten stars in place,
sun, moon, planets,
and all the moons
around the planets,
to call forth bush
and flower
and tree
and set the wind in motion,
to imagine all the animals
and to sculpt them
into life.

All   Six days You worked, Wonder Worker God,
and on the seventh day You rested.

Leader   Six days to create the context
for the last
of your creation,
woman
who seems so much like You,
and man
her mirror image.

All   Six days You worked, Wonder Worker God,
and on the seventh day You rested.

Leader   Blessed are the works of Your hands, O God,
and blessed are all who labor
to bring fullness
from the earth,
all who feed, house, clothe
the cherished fruits
of Your creation.

All   May the work of our hands
and the work of our minds
be reflective of You, our Creator.

    By M. T. Winter, Crossroad Pub. Co., © 1990 Medical Mission Sisters

Leader	Bless all our fields of labor:
	In business and industry,
All	Bless us, O Creator!
Leader	In the healing professions,
All	Bless us, O Creator!
Leader	In commerce, law, and science,
All	Bless us, O Creator!
Leader	In teaching and in research,
All	Bless us, O Creator!
Leader	In the arts and communication,
All	Bless us, O Creator!
Leader	In services and manual labor,
All	Bless us, O Creator!
Leader	In the home and in community
	and in every known arena,
All	Bless us, O Creator!
Leader	Bless all of us who labor hard
	to do Your will, O God,
	to keep Your word,
	prepare Your way,
	and sing Your praise and glory.
All	May the work of our hands
	and the work of our minds
	be reflective of You, our Creator.
Leader	Give us the strength to cope with tensions
	that arise because we are female,
	courage in the face of stereotypes,
	a shield against sexist behavior.
	Give us both competence and humor,
	and a firm belief
	that every new day
	brings a chance to begin again.
All	May the work of our hands
	and the work of our minds
	be reflective of You, our Creator.

By M. T. Winter, Crossroad Pub. Co., © 1990 Medical Mission Sisters

FEMALE SLAVE OF PHILIPPI

◇ **Scripture Reference**   Acts 16:16–24

◇ **Biography**

A female slave with an ability to predict the future has earned vast sums for her masters in Philippi. Her skill is attributed to spirit possession from which she is said to be delivered by Paul. We do not know her name, her age, or her race. We do know that she was owned by men who became furious when she could no longer satisfy their greed, and that she was treated harshly by Paul.

⋄ **Context**

Sorcery or fortune telling was widely practiced in Macedonia and usually involved foretelling the future through the interpretation of various omens or signs. According to the text, the slave was a soothsayer, literally, one who had a Python-spirit, the prophetic spirit of the Delphic oracle. In the Greek Pantheon, Python lived in the earth-womb and knew its secrets, the Delphic oracle had religious significance, and *daimon* was an intimate interior spirit synonymous with "soul." In Jewish culture, soothsaying was considered a sin as serious as idolatry and demons were evil spirits that took possession of people against their will. A clash of religion and culture undoubtedly accompanied the slave's encounter with Paul.

The impetus for the exorcism seems to come more from Paul's own frustration rather than any consideration for the female slave, who may even have been a young girl. What actually happened is uncertain. She may have been delivered of an evil spirit, or the spell binding her to a way of life may simply have been broken. What is clear is that she changed. There is no indication of a religious conversion as a result of this experience, nor concern on Paul's part with regard to her future.

This narrative follows immediately after Paul's association with the well-to-do merchant Lydia. The juxtaposition of these women and their vastly contrasting stories is a point well worth considering.

⋄ **Lectionary Reading**

As we were going to the place of prayer,
we encountered a female slave
who could predict the future
and was making a lot of money for her owners
through fortune telling.
For days she hounded Paul and us, crying,
"These men are servants of the Most High God!
They have come to tell you how to be saved!"
Paul was finally so annoyed
that he turned and said to the spirit,
"I charge you to come out of her
in the name of Jesus Christ."
And the spirit departed.
When her owners saw
that they had lost their source of income,
they seized Paul and Silas
and dragged them to the court in the market place
and accused them before the magistrates:
"These men are Jews who are disturbing our city.
They advocate customs not sanctioned by Rome."
The crowd supported the accusations,
so the magistrates had Paul and Silas stripped
and gave the order for them to be scourged.

After many lashes had been inflicted,
they were thrown into prison,
and the jailer was charged to watch them closely.
He moved them into the inner prison
and secured their feet in the stocks.

◇ **Personal Reflection**

Why do the ghosts
of unresolved pain
come
in the night
unannounced
and remain
to accuse
and abuse,
taking control
of the vulnerable
heart,
violating
the soul.
I have wrestled
with demons
all through the night.
Lord,
let me limp
liberated
into your light.

◇ **Points for Shared Reflection**

- Compare the life stories of Lydia and the female slave and relate this to their experience of the church.

- Do you think the slave was really possessed or was she perhaps clairvoyant and a victim of greed? Were her words to Paul a demonic taunt or a sincere revelation?

- Why was this female of so little consequence to Paul? Was it because her mode of truth-telling was so despicable to a Pharisaic Jew? Was it because of her status? Her gender? Her race?

- What do you suppose happened to her after the incident? How might she have felt about her changed condition? How might she have felt about Christianity?

- In what ways are women's spirit and spirituality misunderstood today?

- Name instances whereby women continue to be held captive by patriarchal systems that exploit and abuse their gifts.

◇ **A Psalm for Women Who Are Abused** (see p. 210)

◇ **Prayer**

You Who hear Your children's cries,
You Whose own Child was abused,
speak from Your warm, compassionate heart
and say to Your wounded daughters:
you are a victim,
you did nothing wrong,
do not let guilt consume you.
Yes, speak from Your warm, compassionate heart
and say to Your wounded daughters:
Shalom of the new fallen snow be with you.
Shalom of the forest path be with you.
Shalom of the singing bird be with you,
now and forever.
Amen.

———— ◇ ————

◇ A PSALM FOR WOMEN WHO ARE ABUSED ◇

Leader   O Sacred Shalom,
we lift to Your compassion
all the victims of abuse
whom we know and do not know.

All   Shalom to Your wounded daughters.

Leader   All women who have been violated
in their bodies
and their spirits.

All   Shalom to Your wounded daughters.

Leader   All who have been exploited
for sex
or greed
or power.

All   Shalom to Your wounded daughters.

Leader   Give them the grace
to shed all guilt
and to shout aloud with Your Spirit:

All   I am a victim!
I did nothing wrong!
I will not let guilt consume me!

Leader   Victims of physical abuse:
All   Do not let guilt consume you.

Leader   Victims of verbal abuse:
All   Do not let guilt consume you.

Leader   Victims of psychological abuse:
All   Do not let guilt consume you.

Leader   Victims of psychotic abuse:
All   Do not let guilt consume you.

Leader   Victims of religious abuse:
All   Do not let guilt consume you.

Leader   Victims of racial abuse:
All   Do not let guilt consume you.

Leader   Victims of society abuse:
All   Do not let guilt consume you.

Leader   May all abused women shout:
All   I am a victim!
I did nothing wrong!
I will not let guilt consume me!

 By M. T. Winter, Crossroad Pub. Co., © 1990 Medical Mission Sisters

Leader	Victims of spouse abuse:
All	Do not let guilt consume you.
Leader	Victims of child abuse:
All	Do not let guilt consume you.
Leader	Victims of sexual abuse:
All	Do not let guilt consume you.
Leader	Victims of rape and incest:
All	Do not let guilt consume you.
Leader	Victims of mind control:
All	Do not let guilt consume you.
Leader	All victims of some form of violence:
All	Do not let guilt consume you.
Leader	May all abused women shout:
All	I am a victim!
	I did nothing wrong!
	I will not let guilt consume me!
	I am a victim!
	I did nothing wrong!
	I will not let guilt consume me!
	I am a victim!
	I did nothing wrong!
	I will not let guilt consume me!

DAMARIS

◇ **Scripture Reference**   Acts 17:22–34

◇ **Biography**

Damaris was a Greek woman who became a Christian after hearing Paul's words before the Areopagus in Athens. She had enough education and intellectual competence to be persuaded by his philosophical argument. No information about her exists, and only recently has there been any speculation about her. The name Damaris appears nowhere else in Greek literature.

◇ **Context**

With Athens, Paul begins a major transition from Macedonia to Greece. Although it was no longer politically prominent, Athens remained an intellectual center. Paul was disturbed by the city's many idols, so he met with Jews and God-fearing Gentiles in the synagogue and held daily debates in the market place. Damaris may have heard him speak in one of these public places prior to his formal speech before the Areopagus.

Intrigued by Paul's perspectives, Epicurean and Stoic philosophers invited him to meet with the Council of the Areopagus, which may have been a court concerned about education. Others would argue that Areopagus was a hill named after the God Ares (Mars Hill), which would place Paul's appearance outdoors before a more general audience. His speech is a Lucan reconstruction, which may accurately represent the original. Form, content, and application reflect good homiletics. Paul's entry point is Athenian worship, and he builds effectively on what is already familiar until he introduces the notion of the resurrection of the body, an element foreign to Greek thought.

Paul was not very successful in Athens, yet he experienced no persecution against him as had happened throughout Macedonia. Among those who accepted Paul's words, two are singled out and these most likely were persons of prominence: Dionysius the Areopagite, to whom later church Fathers and medieval theologians erroneously attributed a number of theological writings, and Damaris, about whom nothing at all has been written.

◇ **Lectionary Reading**

Paul stood before the Council of the Areopagus
and preached the following sermon:
"Citizens of Athens,
I have seen for myself how meticulous you are
in all matters concerning religion.
As I walked around
admiring your sacred monuments,
I noticed an altar inscribed with the words,
'To an Unknown God.'
Well, the God Whom I proclaim to you
is that God you already worship.
Your Unknown God is God our Creator,
Maker of heaven and earth
and everything on the earth,
Who does not live in mortal shrines
of finite construction,
Who is independent of anything
which human hands have made,
for this God is the One who gives life and breath
and everything to everyone.
From one single source,
this God created all who inhabit the earth
and decreed how long each nation should flourish
and determined their boundaries.
God did all of this
so that all might seek the Holy One,
feeling their way toward divinity
until they succeed in finding God.
Yet God is not far from any of us,
for in God we live and move and have our being.
Yes, even your own writers have said,
'We are all God's children.'
Since we are indeed God's children,

we cannot think that God is anything like
the gold, silver, or stone statuary
of human imagination.
God has overlooked such ignorance in the past
but is now saying to everyone everywhere,
it is time to repent.
God has fixed the day of judgment
and one has already been appointed
to judge the world in righteousness.
This person was shown to be God's choice
when God raised him from the dead."
Now when they heard of a resurrection from the dead,
some of them laughed
but others said,
"You must speak of this again."
Paul left them and some followed after him
and they became believers.
Among them were Dionysius the Areopagite
and a woman named Damaris.

◇ **Personal Reflection**

Where survival
depends
upon the whim
of the elements,
wind
rain
sun,
deity is
more
fundamental,
earth
sky
spirit
are one.
Before disparaging
primitive
claims,
examine
our metaphors
and names
for God:
Living Water
Rising Sun
Lord of the Harvest.
Everyone

who acknowledges
needs
knows
Who it is
Who frees
and feeds
and is quick
to rise
to the defense
of God's
generous
providence.

◇ **Points for Shared Reflection**

• What do you suppose became of Damaris after her conversion? There seems to have been no established church in Athens.

• Damaris was obviously well educated and a woman of some prominence. Picture her as the head of a local church, or as a priest, or a preacher, or an itinerant missionary, and add her chapter to the book of Acts by imagining the rest of her story.

• Perhaps Damaris became a believer but was never actually baptized. What might have kept her from joining the church?

• What points are particularly convincing to you as a woman in Paul's Areopagus sermon? Would these points have convinced Damaris?

◇ **A Psalm Praising the Unknown God** (see p. 216)

◇ **Prayer**

O God of Many Names,
we search for names knowing
that no one name can ever reveal You
or contain You or define You.
We know You in a million ways
through all of Your creation,
through Your Spirit gifts within us,
and yet we do not know You,
for You transcend definition
and You live beyond our grasp.
All-Knowing God, Unknown God,
give us wisdom as well as knowledge,
that we might come to know You well
through Your indwelling deep within us
and Your never-failing love. Amen.

———— ◇ ————

Choir 1   All-Knowing God of All Knowledge,
neither You nor we are enamored by
intellectual themes or theories.

All   We have studied all about You
and still we do not know You,
yet we praise You all the same.

Choir 2   All-Wise God of All Wisdom,
subject of ancient philosophies
and modern intuitive trends:

All   We have speculated about You
and still we do not know You,
yet we praise You all the same.

Choir 1   You made the sun and the moon
so that our lives
might be enlightened,
and we know You by their names.

All   O God of the Sun, God of the Moon,
we praise You with these names.

Choir 2   You made the stars and the planets
and revealed to us
their cosmic power,
and we know You by their names.

All   O God of the Stars and Planets,
we praise You with this name.

Choir 1   You made the sea and the surging tides
relentlessly returning,
as a sign of how we return to You,
and we know You by their names.

All   O God of the Sea and the Surging Tide,
we praise You with this name.

Choir 2   You made the trees and forests
ever green and ever growing
with their roots sunk deep within us,
and we know You by their names.

All   O God of Trees and Forests,
we praise You with this name.

Choir 1   You created rainbow colors,
in flowers, fish, butterflies,
and touched the whole of the universe
with the paintbrush of creation,
and we know You by these names.

 By M. T. Winter, Crossroad Pub. Co., © 1990 Medical Mission Sisters

All   O God of Flowers, God of Butterflies,
God of Rainbow Colors,
we praise You with these names.

Choir 2   You orchestrated birdsong,
windsong,
brooksong,
filling the world with music.
and we know You by these names.

All   O God of All Earth's Music,
God of Birdsong,
God of Windsong,
we praise You with these names.

Choir 1   You made all people different,
yet each one in Your image,
and we know You by their names.

All   O God of People,
one by one,
we praise You with our names.

· · · · · · · · · · · · · · · · · · · OPTIONAL · · · · · · · · · · · · · · · · · · ·

Individual*   O God of ___(say your name)___ ,

All   we praise You with our names.

[*Continue to completion of individual naming*]

· ·

Choir 2   O Understanding God Who exceeds all understanding,
You are beyond theologies
and all finite interpretation.

All   We have written of You and defined You
and still we do not know You,
yet we praise You all the same.

Choir 1   O God of Every Religion
yet uncontained by any religion,

Choir 2   the Absolute
transcending every relative doctrinal claim:

All   We worship You, we believe in You,
and still we do not know You,
yet we praise You all the same.

---

*Note: Individual naming is optional. If you elect to do this, let individuals spontaneously choose to participate, or if the group is small, move in turn around the group. If the group is large, you might have all say their names at the same time, and continue on. Give clear directions before beginning the psalm.

PHILIP'S PROPHETIC DAUGHTERS

◊ **Scripture Reference**   Acts 21:8–14

◊ **Biography**

Four women with the gift of prophecy were all daughters of Philip, one of the seven chosen by the apostles in Jerusalem to assist in ministry. The sisters, who never married, lived with their father in Caesarea on the Palestinian coast where they settled after leaving Jerusalem when Stephen was stoned. They are acknowledged by Eusebius the historian as women prophets and transmitters of apostolic tradition whose fame was great in Asia. Much has been recorded in scripture about their father. Nothing has been written about them.

The reference to Philip's prophetic daughters is intriguing. All four are unmarried, which is counter cultural, and in the context of other prophetic utterances, they remain strangely silent. The disciples at Tyre, speaking in the Spirit, beg Paul not to go to Jerusalem (v. 4). At Philip's house, a Judean prophet arrives and repeats the prophetic warning with graphic detail. Did the daughters also speak and were they also ignored? The author of Acts says nothing about the women, yet a later historian will tell of their fame, noting their influence in other places and their prophetic powers. Their gift fulfills the prophecy of Joel which was reiterated by Peter at Pentecost, that women will also prophesy. The prophetic leadership of women was common in Pauline communities and women prophesied in the churches. Paul wrote extensively about this phenomenon in his first letter to the church in Corinth (see chapters 11–14).

◇ **Lectionary Reading**

Our journey from Tyre ended
when we landed at Ptolemais,
where we greeted the community
and stayed with them that day.
The following day we departed
and arrived in Caesarea,
where we went to the house of Philip
the evangelist,
who was one of the seven,
and stayed with him.
Philip had four unmarried daughters
who were prophets.
Several days later,
during our stay,
a prophet named Agabus arrived
from Judea
to see us.
He took Paul's belt,
and with it
he tied up his own hands and feet, saying:
"Thus says the Holy Spirit:
the man to whom this belt belongs
will be bound like this by the Jews in Jerusalem
and handed over to the Gentiles."
On hearing this,
we and the people present
begged Paul not to go to Jerusalem,
but Paul replied:
"What are you hoping to accomplish?

Would you deter me with your tears?
I am ready to go to prison,
ready to die in Jerusalem
for the name of Jesus the Christ."
Paul would not be persuaded,
so we gave up trying and said,
"May God's will be done."

◇ **Personal Reflection**

Wildflowers
God grown
holding their own
tenaciously
on the margins of
upward mobility,
spilling beyond
every boundary,
filling the space
where hope lives
with countless
colorful
alternatives.
To over cultivate
is to kill:
God's growth
flowers
where it will,
living simply
in between
the sterile structures
of routine,
not to be stopped
by stone
or fence
or shrill cries
of impertinence,
reminding all
caught in the chill
of frigid
rigid
ritual:
wildflowers
are first
to break the snow
and by God's grace
the last to go.

◇ **Points for Shared Reflection**

- Would all four female prophets really have remained silent in such a Spirit-charged setting right in their own home? Why would the author of Acts fail to record their participation?

- What is the significance of the four women being unmarried? Was it choice? Circumstance? The consequence of their behavior? Relate this bit of data to the sociology of the times.

- The women were daughters of Philip, but they were first of all daughters of their mother. Who was Philip's wife? Is it possible that she was alive and present during Paul's visit?

- The women were sisters to each other, seemingly of one mind and heart. Reflect on the nurturing nature of such charismatic sisterhood in the broadest sense of the term.

- Where would the daughters have prophesied? Would they ever have gone to Corinth to have met with prophetic sisters there? If so, what would they have learned?

- What prophetic word do you feel compelled to speak to the universal church?

◇ **A Psalm of Prophetic Ministry** (see p. 222)

◇ **Prayer**
Shekinah-Shaddai,
we give You thanks
for Your female power within us,
for courage to speak Your secret word,
grace to put it into practice,
strength to endure the ridicule
and the pressure
of constraint.
Be with us now and always
as we settle ourselves within You,
and visit with grace
the ones we love.
This is the prayer we pray.
Amen.

———— ◇ ————

◇ A PSALM OF PROPHETIC MINISTRY ◇

Leader   Thus says Shaddai:
     my daughters, prophesy!

All   What shall we prophesy?

Leader   Prophesy on love.

All   On that day
     we will feel and know
     the fullness of love
     within us,
     for women will come together
     in a love that spirals outward
     to embrace a global sisterhood
     whose love will welcome all.

Leader   Thus says Shekinah:
     my daughters, prophesy!

All   What shall we prophesy?

Leader   Prophesy on presence.

All   On that day
     no walls will keep
     one person from another,
     and two in one flesh
     will pale before
     the mystery
     of two in one soul and spirit,
     as women,
     fully present,
     herald the presence
     of God.

Leader   Thus says Sophia:
     my daughters, prophesy!

All   What shall we prophesy?

Leader   Prophesy on wisdom.

All   On that day
     the wise will know
     the questions
     to the answers,
     as women make sense
     of all the myths
     from the dreamtime
     of creation
     until the moment after now,

     By M. T. Winter, Crossroad Pub. Co., © 1990 Medical Mission Sisters

	spinning a single story
	from diverse apocrypha.
Leader	Thus says the Spirit:
	my daughters, prophesy!
All	How can we prophesy?
Leader	Prophesy in the Spirit.

.... OPTIONAL ....

All	On that day ...
	[*individuals spontaneously complete the phrase**]*

. . . .

All	On that day
	all flesh will proclaim
	the good news of salvation,
	as women speak their inner truth —
	daughters, sisters, mothers, wives —
	and pray for this gift
	of freedom
	for the men
	who share their lives.

---

*Note: Spontaneous sharing is optional. Give clear directions before beginning the psalm.

By M. T. Winter, Crossroad Pub. Co., © 1990 Medical Mission Sisters   *WomanWord* / **223**

EUODIA AND SYNTYCHE

◇ **Scripture Reference**   Philippians 4:2–3

◇ **Biography**

Two women, Euodia and Syntyche, are mentioned by Paul at the close of his letter to the Philippians, where he states that they worked on an equal basis with him, competing beside him and the rest of his co-workers in the cause of the Gospel. Some disagreement has arisen between the two women, so Paul sends an emissary to help mediate a reconciliation. The nature of the dispute is unknown, but Paul's intervention, which is collegial and not hierarchical, indicates how important the women are both to Paul and to the community in Philippi.

◇ **Context**

At Philippi, both literary and archaeological evidence hint at the community's high regard for women in leadership roles both in and outside Christianity during this period of its history. Euodia and Syntyche most likely are leaders in the church at Philippi, for Paul's response clearly indicates their equality with other church leaders and implies a level of authority and a significant influence there. Paul is probably concerned about the negative impact of their quarrel on the community or even the potential rupture that might result if their personal or public disagreement persists. At stake here are not simply personal agendas but the well-being of the local church and the wider church as well

224

through a unified witness to the Gospel by all who are charged with its proclamation.

◇ **Lectionary Reading**

I appeal to Euodia and
I appeal to Syntyche
to come to an agreement with each other
in Christ.
And I ask you, my colleague,
to be a real companion
and help them to settle this.
For these women have labored beside me
in proclaiming the Gospel
together with Clement
and the others who worked with me
and whose names are in the book of life.

◇ **Personal Reflection**

Inside
my soul
in times
of drought,
I find
my inner secrets
out.
In times
of stress
and raging storm,
pools
of impatience
begin to form:
turn
to where
still waters
run
and don't
spill over
on everyone.

◇ **Points for Shared Reflection**

• Women in leadership positions sometimes compete against each other because the male model of competition is the only one they have known. Has this ever happened to you? To women whom you know? What advice would you offer if you were asked to intervene in such situations?

• Women in leadership positions are often expected to agree with each other on everything. Since women have had little opportunity to air their opinions publicly, differences of opinion are sometimes misunderstood by males as indications of serious dissent. Has this ever happened to you or to women whom you know? How would you handle such a false expectation in a male environment?

- Do you think the two women had a problem or was this really Paul's problem? Why would Paul care so much about what women were saying and about female relationships?

- Reflect some more about Euodia and Syntyche. Who were these women? What were their concerns? What can you say about their worship life and about their experiences in ministry?

◇ **A Psalm of Shared Mission and Ministry** (see p. 227)

◇ **Prayer**

O Holy One of Blessing,
You call us into mission
in a multitude of ways.
Some of us travel around the earth,
some of us tend Your gardens
and Your vineyards
nearer home.
Be with us all
as we struggle to do the ministry
of Your making,
and may we always stay in touch
with the power You place within us
and the peace which Your word proclaims.
May we be there for one another,
and take the time to celebrate time
even as it celebrates us.
Glory and praise to You, Shaddai,
now and forever.
Amen.

———— ◇ ————

◇ A PSALM OF SHARED MISSION AND MINISTRY ◇

Choir 1   We praise You, Shaddai,
and we worship You
with songs that sing of relationship,
with symbols that speak our experience,
with sacraments that celebrate life.

Choir 2   We thank You, Shaddai,
for so many things:
Your promise when we are discouraged,
Your presence when we are lonely,
Your protection when we are attacked.

Choir 1   For You call us and lead us in mission
and strengthen us for our ministry
through the nurturing bonds of community
and the sustaining support of friends.

Choir 2   We are sisters in Your service,
sisters and brothers in Your service,
missionaries in Your service,
wide open to all in need.

Choir 1   We thank You, Shaddai,
and we praise You,
for the challenges and the choices,
for all those who stand beside us,
for all who are there behind us,
for all who have gone before us
to preach and prepare the way.

Choir 2   We thank You, Shaddai,
and we praise You,
rejoicing in all
that we see and hear
of You and Your challenging word;
may we be of one mind in our mission,
work side by side in ministry,
walk hand in hand
through our ups and downs
until You come again.

All   We thank You, Shaddai, and we praise You!
We praise You, Shaddai, and we thank You!
Shower Your blessings upon us
and on all who are touched by our lives.

By M. T. Winter, Crossroad Pub. Co., © 1990 Medical Mission Sisters   *WomanWord* / **227**

PHOEBE

◇ **Scripture Reference**   Romans 16:1–2

◇ **Biography**

Phoebe was a leader in the church at Cenchreae, the seaport city adjacent to Corinth. An official teacher and missionary commended by Paul, she was a woman of authority, responsibility, and influence, and Paul's financial patron. She heads the list of twenty-nine persons greeted by Paul in his letter to the Romans. There is no suggestion of secondary status in Paul's reference to her, but rather a sense of her importance in the community and a hint that others may be subordinate to her.

◇ **Context**

There has been much speculation about Phoebe concerning the precise nature of her role and her relationship to Paul. She is said to be the one who delivered Paul's letter to Rome. If, as Robert Jewett suggests, this letter really was proclaimed orally and interpreted on the spot by the bearer, Phoebe would have had considerable rhetorical skill and experience in theological exposition.

Paul accords her three titles: sister, *diakonos*, *prostatis*. There is growing agreement that "deaconess" is not an accurate translation of *diakonos*, which is the same word Paul uses of himself and other church leaders to indicate equal standing among those who have contributed to the building up of the community, each in their own way. Paul's introduction of Phoebe as "our sister and *diakonos*" parallels that of Timothy as "our brother and God's *diakonos*" (1 Thess 3:2) and Tychicus as "our beloved brother and faithful *diakonos*" (Col 4:7). Traditionally the word, when used to describe men, has been translated "minister" or "missionary," but when applied to Phoebe, a woman, it has been given a subsidiary meaning, such as "deaconess" or "helper."

Until recently, Phoebe was assigned the role of helper to women and children. Now it is presumed she held a leadership position in her church. Phoebe's other title, *prostatis*, is used nowhere else in the New Testament. In other contexts it is taken to mean "leader" or "overseer" and its verb forms confirm this translation. Phoebe is undoubtedly an influential woman. Paul does not question the acceptance of her authority but simply asks that she be treated appropriately. Obviously he is in her debt and is hoping to reciprocate through the hospitality of the churches in Rome.

◇ **Lectionary Reading**

I commend to you our sister Phoebe,
a minister of the church at Cenchreae,
and I ask that in Christ
you extend to her a welcome
that is worthy of the saints.
Give her whatever help she may need from you,
for she has helped a great many people,
and she has been a support to me.

◇ **Personal Reflection**

In the image
of God
we are
created
whole
and even
holy
in the deep
recesses
of the soul,
a prism
absorbing
intimately
the edges
of infinity,
reflecting
it back
imperfectly.
Long

how long
my struggle
to be
the image
of Thou Who
imagined
me,
visible
invisibility,
the skin
of an inner
reality,
icon
of all
creativity
interpreted
intuitively.
Who can understand
the cry
of one
so driven?
Which is why
I stay
inside
and only bless
the existential
loneliness.

◇ **Points for Shared Reflection**

- Imagine that Phoebe has just arrived and you have welcomed her to the community. What questions would you ask her about her personal life and ministry in order to write a more thorough biographical sketch? You might want to form small groups and assign the role of Phoebe to one member of each group. Share and collate your responses.

- What was it like to be a female leader of a first-century church and a colleague of Paul? Compare the ministries of Phoebe, Lydia, and Mary the mother of John Mark (see pp. 195 and 200).

- What is your opinion of Paul with regard to his relationships with women and his overall attitude toward women? What is his relationship to Phoebe? Does this support or challenge your viewpoint?

- In one sense we are all ministers. What is your present ministry and how does it contribute to the mission of the church and/or the mission of Jesus?

◇ **A Psalm of Commissioning for Mission** (see p. 232)

◇ **Prayer**

> You call us, Shaddai,
> and You send us forth
> to the edges of the earth,
> to preach, teach, and minister
> in the world beyond our borders
> and the community beyond the church.
> Whatever our field of service
> or the arena of our mission,
> may we give of ourselves completely
> without stopping to count the cost.
> Commissioned and committed,
> we go in the strength of the Spirit
> to love and serve Shaddai,
> now and forever.
> Amen.

———— ◇ ————

◇ A PSALM OF COMMISSIONING FOR MISSION ◇

Leader The harvest is ready.
 Whom shall I send?

Voice Send me, Shaddai,
 I am ready to serve You,
 all the days of my life.

All Go into the workplace
 and into the streets
 and reveal God's saving Spirit
 through the quality of your life.

Leader The world is waiting.
 Whom shall I send?

Voice Send me, Shaddai,
 I am ready to speak of You,
 all the days of my life.

All Preach the Good News
 by your actions:
 heal, help, teach, touch,
 be of good spirit
 in good times and bad times,
 and live for the glory of God.

Leader The world is hungry.
 Whom shall I send?

Voice Send me, Shaddai,
 I am ready to nourish,
 all the days of my life.

All Feed the hungry
 of body and spirit,
 break the bread of compassion,
 distribute the fragments of hope,
 and be fed by the Word within you.

Leader The vineyard is ready.
 Whom shall I send?

Voice Send me, Shaddai,
 I am ready to work for You,
 all the days of my life.

All Enter into and love the mission
 and your many ministries,
 labor for justice, lobby for peace,
 and may you find contentment
 in the wages of commitment
 when the long hard day is done.

      By M. T. Winter, Crossroad Pub. Co., © 1990 Medical Mission Sisters

PRISCA (PRISCILLA)

◇ **Scripture Reference**   Acts 18:1–3, 18–19, 24–28
1 Corinthians 16:19 / Romans 16:3–5
2 Timothy 4:19

◇ **Biography**

Prisca or Priscilla, a Latin Christian of noble birth, and her husband Aquila, a Jewish convert and tentmaker by trade, exercised a team ministry, led a church that met at their house, and were considered co-workers of Paul, who lived with them for eighteen months while they were in exile in Corinth. They accompanied Paul to Ephesus and when he left, they remained there and took on the task of instructing Apollos in the specifics of the Christian faith. Paul was deeply indebted to them and they were well known to the Pauline churches. They established house churches in three cities: Corinth, Ephesus, and Rome. Four of the six times their names appear in scripture, Prisca is mentioned first, and when Paul sends greetings to the couple, he greets Prisca before Aquila, a sure sign of her prominence in a culture where this is contrary to social mores.

◇ **Context**

Prisca and Aquila are a model of team ministry and prominent in the house church movement of first-century Christianity. A church meets in the couple's house wherever they happen to settle. In the list of greetings in Romans 16, theirs is the only group that is designated "church" (*ekklesia*). The texts establish Prisca as a church leader, a missionary apostle, and a teacher of a missionary apostle. Paul considers her a co-worker, referring to her and her husband as *synergos*, "fellow worker," the same designation he uses of himself and others he considers ministers of the Gospel, a list which includes, among others, Timothy, Apollos, Mark, Luke, and two other women, Euodia and Syntyche.

Paul is grateful to Prisca and her husband for risking their necks on his behalf. They probably did endanger their lives interceding for him with the authorities, an indication of their influential status. However, Robert Jewett suggests that the phrase might also hint at their Roman citizenship, for only citizens had the right to die by decapitation. The death penalty for others was crucifixion or the wild beasts of the Arena. There is no suggestion of subordination in Prisca's relationship to Paul or to her husband. She is clearly their equal and Paul seems to take this significant fact for granted. The lectionary reading that follows is a composite of all related texts.

◇ **Lectionary Reading**

After this Paul left Athens
and went to Corinth,
where he met a Jew named Aquila
whose family came from Pontus.
He and his wife Priscilla
had recently left Italy
because an edict of the emperor Claudius
had expelled all the Jews from Rome.
Paul went to visit them
and when he discovered they were tentmakers,
the same trade as his own,
he stayed with them
and they worked together.
Every sabbath he held debates
in the synagogue
to convert both Jews and Greeks.

After some time
Paul took leave of the community
and sailed for Syria,
accompanied by Priscilla and Aquila.
At Cenchreae he had his hair cut
because of a vow he had made.
When they reached Ephesus,
he left them.

One day an Alexandrian Jew named Apollos

came to Ephesus.
He was eloquent,
well versed in scripture,
and although he had been instructed
in the Way
and preached with spiritual fervor
and was accurate in all that he taught
about Jesus,
he had only experienced the baptism
of John.
He spoke boldly in the synagogue,
and when Priscilla and Aquila heard him,
they took an interest in him
and they taught him more
about the Way.
When Apollos considered
going over to Achaia,
the community encouraged him
and wrote to the disciples there,
asking them to welcome him.
When he arrived, he was able,
by the grace of God,
to help and support the believers
because of the energetic way
he refuted all his opponents
and demonstrated from the scriptures
that Jesus was the Christ.

From Paul's Letter to Corinth:
The churches of Asia send greetings.
Aquila and Prisca,
together with the church
that meets at their house,
send you warmest greetings in Christ.

From Paul's Letter to Rome:
My greetings to Prisca and Aquila,
my co-workers in Christ Jesus,
who risked their necks
to save my life,
to whom, not only I,
but all the churches of the Gentiles
owe a debt of gratitude.
My greetings also
to the church that meets at their house.

From the Second Letter to Timothy:
Greetings to Prisca and Aquila
and the household of Onesiphorus.

◇ **Personal Reflection**

Out of the cosmic
chaos
the theme arises:
generations
of tears
tyranny
tension
suspension of meaning
measure
the beat of the universe
alter
the song.
Small variations
of healing
and hope
offer cacophony
counterpoint
giving some days
harmony
for the heart's helplessness:
primitive praise.

◇ **Points for Shared Reflection**

- Prisca and Aquila seem ideal role models for a female/male team ministry. From the little we know of their lives, what do you suppose enables them to function so effectively and so harmoniously?

- Why have we heard so little about Prisca and Aquila if they were so prominent and so effective?

- What would it take for an effective and harmonious female/male team ministry today? Do you feel drawn toward such a ministry, lay or otherwise? If so, what kind of ministry, where, and with whom?

- House churches were normative in the early years of a developing Christianity. Have you ever been part of a house church? If so, reflect on that experience and share some of its strengths and some of its weaknesses.

- If you have never been part of a house church but think you would like to be, what kind of a church would you want in terms of people, structure, ritual, commitment, community, and social action?

◇ **A Psalm of Partnership in Ministry** (see p. 238)

◇ **Prayer**

> We thank You, O God Within and Beyond us,
> for linking our lives
> in so many ways,
> making a chain of hope
> and compassion
> long enough
> and strong enough
> to circle the globe.
> When we walk hand in hand,
> when we work side by side,
> the impossible becomes
> the next challenge before us,
> and we know we can do
> what we dared not attempt.
> May mountains of misery melt
> with Your Word of concern
> which we put into action,
> and may there never again
> be despair or denial
> of Your saving grace.
> Amen.

———— ◇ ————

◇ A PSALM OF PARTNERSHIP IN MINISTRY ◇

Choir 1   We are partners in the mystery
                 of redemption,
             partners in the mystery
                 of reconciliation,
             partners in the misery
                 of the world's population,
             partners in the way
                 of the cross.

Choir 2   We are partners in the ministry
                 of service,
             partners in the ministry
                 of justice and peace,
             partners in the liturgy
                 of church
                 and life,
             partners in healing
                 and hope.

Choir 1   Together we reach out to touch
             the untouchables.

Choir 2   Together we move out to teach
             the taught.

Choir 1   Together we stand up to preach
             right practice.

Choir 2   Together we practice
             what we preach.

Choir 1   Ours is the gift of good company
             on days
             when there's nobody else there
             beside us.

Choir 2   Ours is the gift of affirming
             the ways
             of the God Who is working
             within us.

Choir 1   Blessed is the partnership rooted
             in love
             that spills over,
             spreads over,
             covers over everything
             negative
             and uninspiring.

    By M. T. Winter, Crossroad Pub. Co., © 1990 Medical Mission Sisters

Choir 2   Blessed is the fellowship
partnership shares
with its circle
of friends
and supporters.

Choir 1   God of Relationship,
bless this relationship,
strengthen this partnership,
deepen this fellowship,
let it be symbol of Your
mode of Being
and sign of Your own
noncompetitive ways.

Choir 2   God of Companionship,
may we be supportive,
may we be effective,
bringing to life all the best
in each other
so that we might help others
see good in themselves.

All   Thank You, O God, for the gift
and the grace
of partnership
in the mystery
of living.

By M. T. Winter, Crossroad Pub. Co., © 1990 Medical Mission Sisters

WOMEN IN MINISTRY IN ROME:

Julia, Junia, Mary, Persis, Tryphena, Tryphosa, Sister of Nereus, Mother of Rufus (and Phoebe and Prisca)

◇ **Scripture Reference**   Romans 16:1–16

◇ **Biography**

Ten of the twenty-nine persons mentioned by Paul in the final chapter of his letter to Rome are women. All are Paul's co-workers in the ministry of the church. Prisca (Priscilla) is referred to in two other letters and in the Book of Acts. None of the other women are mentioned anywhere else in the New Testament. What follows is all we know of the eight women we remember here. For information on Phoebe and Prisca, see pp. 228 and 233.

Mary, Persis, Tryphena, Tryphosa
All four are said to have "worked very hard." Paul uses the Greek verb *kopaio* ("to work very hard") to refer to a ministry of the Gospel and to describe his own apostolic ministry. It is a word associated with preaching and evangelism and a leadership which commands authority. These four women to whom Paul sends greetings were engaged in such a ministry in Rome. Paul adds a dimension to his greeting to Persis. He calls her "friend." It has been suggested that Tryphena and Tryphosa might have been sisters because of their like-sounding names.

Julia
She is greeted without comment. In a study of names in early Roman records, the name Julia was found more than 1400 times. It was a common Latin name for slaves and other members of the Julian households. Some scholars would pair Julia with Philologus as his wife.

Junia
This woman is hard to find in most English translations of the Bible because the name appears as the male name Junias, and it is assumed that this person was a man. Two explanations have been offered for this mistaken identity. One is clearly grammatical. The direct object of the Greek verb "to greet" is *Junian*, the same form for both female and male. However, records reveal that Junia was a common female name in the Roman Empire of that time. There is verification of its use as a woman's name more than 250 times, but there is no evidence at all of its use among males.

This leads into the second and probably real reason for the shift in gender, the fact that Paul calls Junia an apostle. One of the Greek Fathers of the church, John Chrysostom (d. 407), not known for his affirmation of women, knew Junia was a woman and was amazed that she should be called an apostle. The earliest evidence of the shift to Junias, the male form, appears in the thirteenth-century writings of Aegidius of Rome (says scholar Bernadette Brooten), and the practice has been continued ever since. Paul referred to Andronicus and Junia as outstanding apostles, the only instance where he specifically identified someone besides himself and the twelve as apostles. It has been suggested that Andronicus was Junia's husband and the two were engaged in a team ministry similar to that of Prisca and Aquila. Both suffered imprisonment and both shared a bond with Paul.

Sister of Nereus

Nereus was a Greek name given to slaves particularly in Rome. As a family member, the sister of a slave would have shared the same social status. Paul greeted her without comment and without naming her, indicating she had probably been referred to him through someone else. She must have been important to the church in Rome or Paul would not have sent greetings.

Mother of Rufus

Paul knew the mother of Rufus who had been a mother to him too at one time, and his greeting to her was warm. Perhaps he did not name her because he thought of her as a mother. He characterized her son as someone special, a chosen servant of Christ. Tradition has it that he was the same Rufus whom Mark described as the son of Simon of Cyrene (15:21). That would make his mother the wife of the man who helped Jesus carry his cross.

◇ **Context**

We are just beginning to realize how much this list of names adds to our understanding of Paul's letter to the Romans. Chapter 16 is now considered a vital part of the letter, for it tells us to whom the letter was addressed. Scholars have identified five different house churches and a number of unattached individuals among those listed. Three women were associated with groups. Prisca had a church at her house. Julia and the sister of Nereus belonged to another group.

The significance of this information has only recently come to light. The emperor Claudius expelled all Jews from Rome in A.D. 49 because of disturbances within synagogues arising from disputes between Christians and Jews. During the five years of exile, Jewish-Christian groups were deprived of Jewish leadership. In the interim, Gentile leaders took over and the house church movement continued to grow. Paul met a number of Jewish refugees in exile, among them Prisca and Aquila, and no doubt others on the Romans list. Prisca probably gave Paul the names of other women leaders in Rome with whom he was not yet familiar. When the ban was lifted and the Jews returned, many had difficulty assimilating with already established groups. Paul addressed his letter to these church leaders in Rome, ten of whom were women, some attached to house churches, some still unattached, as a call to unity in Christ, hoping for their collaborative support of his forthcoming mission to Spain.

◇ **Lectionary Reading**

I commend to you our sister Phoebe,
a minister of the church at Cenchreae,

and I ask that in Christ
you extend to her a welcome
that is worthy of the saints.
Give her whatever help she may need from you,
for she has helped a great many people,
and she has been a support to me.

My greetings to Prisca and Aquila,
my co-workers in Christ Jesus,
who risked their necks
to save my life,
to whom, not only I,
but all the churches of the Gentiles
owe a debt of gratitude.
My greetings also
to the church that meets at their house.

Greetings to my friend Epaenetus,
Asia's first convert for Christ.

Greetings to Mary,
who has worked so hard among you.

Greetings to Andronicus and Junia,
those outstanding apostles,
my compatriots and fellow prisoners,
who were Christians before I was.

Greetings to Ampliatus,
my friend in the Lord;
to Urban, my fellow worker in Christ;
to my friend Stachys;
to Apelles who has gone through so much
for Christ;
to everyone who belongs to the household
of Aristobulus;
to my compatriot Herodion;
to those in the household of Narcissus
who belong to Christ.

Greetings to Tryphena and Tryphosa,
who work hard for Christ.

Greetings to my friend Persis,
who has also worked hard for Christ.

Greetings to Rufus,
a chosen servant for Christ,

and to his mother,
who has been a mother to me.

Greetings to Asyncritus, Phlegon, Hermes,
Patrobas, Hermas, and all the faithful
who are with them.

Greetings to Philologus, Julia,
Nereus and his sister,
and Olympas,
and all the saints who are with them.

Greet each other with a holy kiss.
All the churches of Christ send greetings.

◇ **Personal Reflection**

It caught me
by surprise:
the lighthearted
lilt of your laughter
I've come to know well,
but I wasn't prepared
for the depth of the pain
I perceived
when I looked
in your eyes.

◇ **Points for Shared Reflection**

- Select one of the women on the Romans list. What is there about her life or ministry that is of particular interest to you? Can you identify something in her life that relates to something in yours?

- They tried to erase Junia from the list and replace her with a male because the church could not imagine a woman as an apostle. Do you think there were other female apostles in the early Christian church?

- Do you think Jesus might have called females into his apostolic circle and that their names also have been erased? What reasons do you give to support your views?

- The ten women in ministry in Rome may well have formed their own support group similar to today's women-church. What are some of the concerns they might have shared with one another? What would you like to share with this group now?

- How vital is it for an individual to be part of a community or local church? Do you feel supported and at home in the local church with which you are affiliated or the group to which you belong?

◇ **A Psalm for Remembering Women** (see p. 246)

◇ **Prayer**

O One Who Welcomes Women
into the household of the Spirit
and the leadership of the church,
be with all women
who feel themselves
on the outside, looking in,
kept far from the banquet table
richly laden with Your blessings
and intended for us all.
May Your symbols of abundance
not be used to mock our poverty.
Throw open the doors that bar us from
our share of daily bread.
May the strength of female apostles
reach to us across the ages,
and the wisdom of our longing match
the folly of Your cross.
Wise Woman God,
Tender Woman God,
You are the One Who holds us all
in the hope of Your new tomorrow
and the faith of Your yesterday.
Amen.

———— ◇ ————

◇ A PSALM FOR REMEMBERING WOMEN ◇

Leader   For the times you walked the city streets
            and ministered to the homeless:
All   Julia, Junia, Mary, Persis,
            we remember you.

Leader   For the times you preached the word of God:
All   Julia, Junia, Mary, Persis,
            we remember you.

Leader   For the times you opened your home to others:
All   Julia, Junia, Mary, Persis,
            we remember you.

Leader   For leading the church through its infancy:
All   Julia, Junia, Mary, Persis,
            we remember you.

Leader   For the years you spent in exile
            disassociated from your roots:
All   Tryphena and Tryphosa,
            we remember you.

Leader   For the years you worked hard for the gospel:
All   Tryphena and Tryphosa,
            we remember you.

Leader   For the times you were excluded
            from the community life you cherished:
All   Tryphena and Tryphosa,
            we remember you.

Leader   For the times you gave yourselves to others:
All   Tryphena and Tryphosa,
            we remember you.

Leader   For the freedom you brought to other women:
All   Sister of Nereus, mother of Rufus,
            we remember you.

Leader   For the women and men you nourished
            and nurtured:
All   Sister of Nereus, mother of Rufus,
            we remember you.

Leader   For the centuries you were forgotten
            when male leaders were remembered:
All   Sister of Nereus, mother of Rufus,
            we remember you.

    By M. T. Winter, Crossroad Pub. Co., © 1990 Medical Mission Sisters

Leader	For having to enter communities now where nobody knows your name:
All	Sister of Nereus, mother of Rufus, we remember you.
Leader	Whenever I walk the city streets and am devastated by the homeless:
All	Julia, Junia, Mary, Persis, please remember me.
Leader	When I try to give myself to others:
All	Tryphena and Tryphosa, please remember me.
Leader	Whenever I feel forgotten in the company of male leaders:
All	Sister of Nereus, mother of Rufus, please remember me.
Leader	All of our sisters, known and unknown, who ministered in the church of Rome, who were leaders in the church of Rome, remember your sisters who are or have been devastated by the church of Rome.
All	Julia, Junia, Mary, Persis, Tryphena and Tryphosa, sister of Nereus, mother of Rufus, Phoebe and Priscilla: remember us, your sisters. And pray for the church of Rome.

By M. T. Winter, Crossroad Pub. Co., © 1990 Medical Mission Sisters

NYMPHA

◇ **Scripture Reference**   Colossians 4:15

◇ **Biography**

Nympha was a Christian woman of Asia Minor to whom Paul sent greetings at the close of his letter to the Colossians. The local church in Laodicea (although some would say in Colossae) met at her house.

◇ **Context**

Laodicea was situated in the southwest corner of Phrygia on the ancient highway leading up from Ephesus and through the Lycus Valley (the site of the city) into Syria. It stood just ten miles to the west of Colossae. There was considerable exchange between the churches of both cities. Paul closes his letter to the Colossians with the directive that this letter be shared with the community at Laodicea and that their letter (no longer extant) be obtained and read at Colossae. When Paul greets Nympha at the close of his Colossian letter, it is not clear just where her home is located and a case could be made for either city.

There is a long history of disagreement about the gender of the person named, since the Greek accusative form (*Nymphan*) can mean a man (*Nymphas*) or a woman (*Nympha*). Syriac and Egyptian translations favor the feminine and adjust the corresponding pronoun to "her." Western and Byzantine texts consider the person to be male and the pronoun in these translations is "his." Feminist scholarship concludes that the masculine form was a correction of the original female name, since it was inconceivable that a woman should hold such a position of leadership. Because of this gender confusion, and in many instances gender discrimination, Nympha's name does not appear in some traditional commentaries nor in a recent anthology of New Testament women.

◇ **Lectionary Reading**

Give my greetings
to the community at Laodicea
and to Nympha
and the church
which meets in her house.

◇ **Personal Reflection**

The pompoms
of papyrus
swamps
swell
and sway
majestically,
a link
to ancient
history,
and in their
wildly waving
zeal,
one can imagine
chariot wheel
and proud
olympic
pageantry,
hear
in their
soliloquies
critique
of past
philosophies,

catch
in their excitement
hint
of Homer
and Septuagint.
Framed against
the fading light,
feather fingered
fronds
invite
from me
the books
I've yet to write.

◇ **Points for Shared Reflection**

• The religious climate of Colossae and Laodicea was influenced by a strong interest in celestial and cosmic powers. Using information embedded in the Colossian letter, imaginatively reconstruct the character of the church that met at Nympha's house.

• There is still a strong interest in astrology, and many people today consult their horoscope for a sense of direction. Is there any connection between these orientations and Christian spirituality?

• What might have been the style, emphases, components of a liturgy led by Nympha? How might her liturgy have differed from that of Mary in her house church in Jerusalem? Or Lydia in Philippi? Or our own?

◇ **A Psalm to the Cosmic Christa** (see p. 251)

◇ **Prayer**

Holy One of Blessing,
You are the One Whom people praise,
even without their knowing,
for You are God of the Universe,
and traces of Your passing by
still blaze in the cosmic corridors
and push us past the stars.
O Life of All Living Matter,
Organic Solicitude,
draw us toward that which is vital,
infuse us with a singular eye
so that all we perceive will be image of You
and Your cosmic beatitude.
Holy One of Blessing,
here and now we praise You. Amen.

———— ◇ ————

◇ A PSALM TO THE COSMIC CHRISTA ◇

Leader   O Holy One of Blessing,
You gave birth to a universe
and universal blessings,
created an environment
of freedom
in which to grow:

All   We gather to remember this,
until You come again.

Leader   O Holy One of Blessing,
You made us in Your image,
fruitful and productive,
a replica of womb-love
and compassion
for all:

All   We gather to remember this,
until You come again.

Leader   O Holy One of Blessing,
You feed us
with Your substance,
lifting our hungry spirits
to Your charismatic breasts:

All   We gather to remember this,
until You come again.

Leader   O Holy One of Blessing,
You welcome all
who turn to You
and embrace the ill-begotten:

All   We gather to remember this,
until You come again.

Leader   O Holy One of Blessing,
You spill Your blood
upon the earth
to mark the periodic pause
within Your fruitfulness:

All   We gather to remember this,
until You come again.

Leader   O Holy One of Blessing,
You write our sacred stories,
charting the course of life
and death
in tender narrative:

By M. T. Winter, Crossroad Pub. Co., © 1990 Medical Mission Sisters

All	We gather to remember this, until You come again.
Leader	O Holy One of Blessing, O Blessed Hospitality, embracing every race and every culture, as Your own:
All	We gather to remember this, until You come again.
Leader	O Holy One of Blessing, You integrate all wisdom in a single song of glory, summing up all global praise:
All	We gather to remember this, until You come again.
Leader	O Holy One of Blessing, those seeking You will find You, for You are both the Seeker and the One Who Would Be Found:
All	We gather to remember this, until You come again.
Leader	O Holy One of Blessing, in You is all convergence of mystery and meaning:
All	We gather to remember this, until You come again.

By M. T. Winter, Crossroad Pub. Co., © 1990 Medical Mission Sisters

APPHIA

◇ **Scripture Reference**   Philemon 1–3

◇ **Biography**

Apphia is greeted by Paul at the beginning of his letter to Philemon. She, Philemon, and Archippus are members of a house church or churches in the Lycus Valley, either at Colossae or Laodicea.

◇ **Context**

Paul's letter to Philemon is addressed to three persons: Philemon, Apphia, and Archippus. Since the second century it has been assumed that Apphia was the wife of Philemon, who was in charge of the church in their house, and the mother of Archippus. Most writers presume that all three were members of the same church, which was located in Colossae. It has also been suggested that both men had churches, that Philemon, head of all the Lycus Valley churches, was located in Laodicea and Archippus in Colossae.

If two churches are a reasonable possibility, why not three? Instead of a family relationship, why not a collegial one, with each in charge of a separate house church? Or if not three churches, a team leadership of the church in their house? Traditional commentaries have not explored the possibilities for women in ministry. We meet Apphia parenthetically, in the opening lines of a letter concerning Onesimus, a former slave, probably to Philemon, whom Paul loves as his "very heart." Paul hopes for his full freedom and encourages his swift return. Whatever the relationship between the recipients of the letter, whether family or colleagues in the ministry, one can presume that Apphia participated in the decision concerning the former slave.

◇ **Lectionary Reading**

From Paul, a prisoner
for Jesus Christ,
and from Timothy our brother,
to Philemon our beloved fellow worker,
and Apphia our sister,
and Archippus our fellow soldier,
and the church that meets in your house:
Grace and peace to you from God
and from Jesus, God's anointed.

◇ **Personal Reflection**

Now
nearly night,
a lone lamp's
light
lingers
and fingers
an interlude
of temporary
solitude.
Blest
is this
precious time
between
a diligent day's
burnt offering
and the stringent
pungent
praise
of kerosene.

◇ **Points for Shared Reflection**

- Although Apphia's name has been recorded, her personality and her contribution as wife, mother, leader in the church remain anonymous. Discuss how and why this is still true of women's reality today.

- If the three were team leaders of a house church in Asia Minor, what might have been Apphia's role and some of her contributions, and why?

- What are some of the things Apphia might have said concerning the freeing of Onesimus the slave? Name some ways in which women today share a common bondage with both of them.

◇ **A Psalm for Affirming Identity** (see p. 256)

◇ **Prayer**

O Blessed "I Am,"
God of the Universe,
give us a sense of identity
as Your children,
as Your people,
as Your partners,
as Your friends.
Help us to know You
and to know ourselves
in relationship to You.
May we present ourselves in such a way
that all will know for certain
that you are our God
and we are Yours
now and forever.
Amen.

---- ◇ ----

Choir 1   Who do people say we are?
Wife? Mother? Sister? Daughter?

Choir 2   Women, who do *we* say we are?

Choir 1   Partner to our Sister-God
in the first flush of creation,
sharing the splendor,
sharing the pain
of building a new tomorrow.

Choir 2   Colleague of our Creator-God
in every new beginning,
firm as the everlasting hills
in the faith we are guided by.

Choir 1   Who do people say we are?
Wife? Mother? Sister? Daughter?

Choir 2   Women, who do *we* say we are?

Choir 1   Mother of mercy who lives the role
of caretaker of creation,
dressing the wounds of battered belief
on the eve of a nuclear night.

Choir 2   Mothers of mothers who age and die
and return to our Primeval Mother,
maternally drawn to every cry
of discomfort and human need.

Choir 1   Who do people say we are?
Wife? Mother? Sister? Daughter?

Choir 2   Women, who do *we* say we are?

Choir 1   Sister to the sensuous sea
that ebbs and flows
through the ages,
linking the life within us
to the lives that are all around.

Choir 2   Sister to the silent song
that sings of a new day dawning,
full up and spilling over
with its polyrhythmic praise.

Choir 1   Who do people say we are?
Wife? Mother? Sister? Daughter?

Choir 2   Women, who do *we* say we are?

By M. T. Winter, Crossroad Pub. Co., © 1990 Medical Mission Sisters

Choir 1	Daughter of the Living God, daughter of My Mother, shaped like a sacred icon in the image of Her embrace.
Choir 2	Daughter of the Daughter of God, the Christa of the New Creation, in Whom we rise above all attempts to dull or destroy the dream.
Choir 1	Who do *people* say we are?
Choir 2	We are who *we* say we are!
All	May the blessings of God be with all women. Praise to You, El Shaddai.

By M. T. Winter, Crossroad Pub. Co., © 1990 Medical Mission Sisters

CHLOE

◇ **Scripture Reference**   1 Corinthians 1:10–11

◇ **Biography**

Chloe is mentioned in Paul's first letter to the Corinthians as the source of Paul's awareness of dissension within the church. Chloe's people have told him about it. She may have been the leader of a house church. Paul knows Chloe well enough to trust the word of her representatives, but she remains unknown to us.

◇ **Context**

The seriousness of the dissension among various factions within the Corinthian community led Paul to write a letter to the church he had founded. After Paul had left Corinth, strong personal loyalties to representatives of different aspects of Christianity were beginning to divide the church. Apollos, a Palestinian Jew and eloquent orator, probably appealed to the better educated minority. Jewish Christians who had emigrated from Palestine and Syria were particularly attached to Peter. The majority claimed they belonged to Paul. The phrase, "I belong to Christ," may have been the boast of the pneumatic or charismatic groups or the Judaizers who had known Jesus personally and now challenged Paul's apostolic authority. Also present were those with gnostic tendencies, as well as "the weak" who were scrupulous and easily prone to scandal.

It apparently escalated to the point where Chloe in desperation sent word to Paul to do something about it. Or if Chloe was living in Ephesus where Paul received the disturbing news, as has also been suggested, then her associates in Corinth acted on their own initiative. Precisely who Chloe's people were is uncertain. The phrase may mean family, servants, friends, or members of a church which met in her house. The lectionary reading includes some sense of the scope of the dissension (and extends to verses 12–13, 17, 31).

◇ **Lectionary Reading**

I appeal to you,
my brothers and my sisters,
for the sake of Jesus Christ,
to settle your differences.
Instead of disagreeing among yourselves,
be united again in belief
and in practice.
It has been told to me
by Chloe's people
that there are serious dissensions among you.
What I mean are all those slogans you use,
such as, "I belong to Paul,"
"I belong to Apollos,"
"I belong to Cephas,"
"I belong to Christ."
Is Christ divided?
Was Paul crucified for you?
Were you baptized in the name of Paul?
Christ did not send me to baptize
but to preach the good news of the Gospel.
As the scripture says,
"If anyone wants to boast,
let that person boast about Christ."

◇ **Personal Reflection**

Holy
holy the Ground
of Being
seeing
freeing me
lifting me
higher
returning
turning me
to the Fire.

- From your sense of the situation in Corinth, who do you think were "Chloe's people"?

- Since women were very involved in the life of the Corinthian church, which of the many gifts named by Paul (1 Cor 11–14) might Chloe have received and how would she have expressed that gift in worship?

- The Corinthian dissension is sometimes reflected in the women's movement of our own experience, where one is liberal, another is conservative, one is pro-life, the other pro-choice, one is a feminist, and so on. How can women preserve a unity amid so much diversity?

- Women are particularly disturbed by situations of disintegration. Is there a divisive reality in your life that corresponds to the Corinthian situation? What is needed to bring about a reconciliation?

◇ **A Psalm for Healing Divisions** (see p. 261)

◇ **Prayer**

Living God,
Loving God,
You are the source
of all that is,
and all that is
is holy
when it seeks itself in You.
You are the bond
that unites us all
and erases all division.
May we be one
as You are one in us
and we in You.
Amen.

———— ◇ ————

◇ A PSALM FOR HEALING DIVISIONS ◇

Choir 1   O God, You are One,
eternally One,
One God of all earth's people.

Choir 2   You give birth
to all Your children,
and You know us each by name.

Choir 1   Yet time after time,
we name You
and claim You
as though You were
our God only,
defining infinity
everywhere
by finite limitations
to fit our sacred shrines.

Choir 2   Around the world,
which You know well,
we run from one another
to the refuge
of our religions,
citing our sacred scriptures
as our children
go to war.

All   Heal, O God, all divisions
caused by the rules
of our religions.
May our rituals
and our theologies
proclaim that You are One.

Choir 1   O God, You are Life.
There is only one Life,
one Source of all our living,

Choir 2   yet we can live life
religiously
in many different ways.

Choir 1   All that God is,
all that God does
is meant to be a blessing.

Choir 2   All that we do
and are
should be a blessing
in Her name.

Choir 1	God is Love.
	There is only one Love,
	one Source of all our loving,
Choir 2	yet we can live Love's reality
	by many other names.
Choir 1	The love of a lover,
	a parent,
	a child,
	a sibling,
	a friend,
	a mystic:
Choir 2	all are one,
	for all love is one
	in the Love
	love lives
	inside.
All	Heal, O God, all divisions
	caused by our empty attempts
	at loving,
	and may every graced encounter
	be for each of us
	sacrament.

  By M. T. Winter, Crossroad Pub. Co., © 1990 Medical Mission Sisters

CLAUDIA

◇ **Scripture Reference**   2 Timothy 4:21

◇ **Biography**

Greetings are sent to Timothy from a woman named Claudia. All we really know about her is her name.

◇ **Context**

Claudia does not even appear in some commentaries, and in the present push to recover women's lost history, almost nothing is written of her. Claudia was the subject of conjecture in the early centuries of the church. According to one tradition recorded in the *Apostolic Constitutions* (VII.46), she was the wife of Pudens, a Roman senator converted by Peter, and also the mother of Linus who succeeded Peter as bishop of Rome. If the letter to Timothy was indeed written by Paul while he was in prison in Rome, then we can presume Claudia lived in that city. However, authorship of the letter is uncertain, so we cannot really locate her there. Since so much of what we know is speculative, it might be helpful to look upon her simply as Everywoman, a historical figure lost to us now in the silence of the centuries. Perhaps if we sit with her for awhile, her spirit will speak directly to us.

Do your best to come before winter.
Ebulus sends greetings to you,
as do Pudens
and Linus
and Claudia
and all the community of believers.

◇ **Personal Reflection**

Held
in the hollow
of the everlasting
hills,
filled
with a vision
of paradise
found,
how green
the valley
with cattle
and sheep,
the patchwork
quilt
on the opposite
slope,
the steep
sure ascent
of terraced
hope.
Sound
distilled
and amplified,
pulsates
with life
as the mist
descends.
Another day
ends.
Another moon
rises.
Love,
how I love
your many
disguises.

- The trinity of names suggests a family circle or a team leadership for the community of believers. Sit for awhile in silence and let Claudia speak to you. Who does she say she was?

- If Claudia can be anything we imagine her to be, then we can be anyone we imagine us to be. Who would you like to be as a woman today, and why?

- So much of women's reality has been lost to history because their stories have gone unrecorded. What are you doing to ensure that the same will not be said of the women of our times?

◇ **A Psalm for Everywoman** (see p. 266)

◇ **Prayer**

O God of Many Names
and marvelous deeds,
day after day
we Your people
gather to remember You.
Help us recover
all the lost lives
of those who are long forgotten,
those who have lived
to proclaim Your word
and to prepare the Way for us.
Let us not take lightly
all that dedicated service.
Let us learn from past example
how to shape our present times,
through You and in You.
Amen.

———— ◇ ————

◇ A PSALM FOR EVERYWOMAN ◇

Choir 1   Who will retrieve our stories
from the void of the unremembered?

Choir 2   Who will believe we were who we are
and did all the things we do?

Choir 1   I have seen women breaking bread
and taking the cup of salvation.

Choir 2   I have heard women preaching the word
and teaching theology.

Choir 1   I have met women in mission abroad,
restructuring church and society.

Choir 2   I have met women here at home
doing much of the same.

Choir 1   I have sung songs that women have written,
but seldom in church on Sunday.

Choir 2   I have even prayed to my Mother God,
but not in the sacred rites.

Choir 1   Where are the books to record the deeds
of the prophets of the present?

Choir 2   Where are the ones who will keep and preserve
the truth of women's ways?

Choir 1   Who will take the time we have taken
to find the lost lives of our sisters?

Choir 2   Who will seek us and find us?
Who will remember our names?

                         By M. T. Winter, Crossroad Pub. Co., © 1990 Medical Mission Sisters

PAUL'S SISTER

◇ **Scripture Reference**   Acts 23:12–22

◇ **Biography**

While Paul was in prison in Jerusalem, "the son of Paul's sister" learned of a plot to ambush his uncle and intervened to prevent his assassination. We know nothing at all about the young man's mother.

◇ **Context**

When Paul was speaking in Jerusalem, the people became enraged. They accused him of preaching against Judaism and the Law and of desecrating the temple. An agitated mob wanted to lynch him, but Roman soldiers intervened and led him away in chains. Under cross-examination, Paul revealed his Roman citizenship. The tribune was horrified to learn that he had put a Roman citizen in chains. Thanks to Paul's nephew, his sister's son, the tribune learned of a plot to assassinate Paul and decided to send him at once to the procurator in Caesarea. Under cover of darkness, heavily guarded by a contingent of soldiers, Paul safely escaped from Jerusalem.

Nothing is known about Paul's family or what they thought of his conversion to the Way. His nephew most likely was a Jew in order to have known about the conspiracy, or perhaps he overheard someone speak of it, or his mother may have had connections with the religious hierarchy. This reference to Paul's sister and her son may represent a tradition that Paul grew up in Jerusalem. Twice Paul mentions having lived in the city, once as a student of Gamaliel (Acts 22:3; 26:4).

◇ **Lectionary Reading**

Paul's enemies held a secret meeting,
and they vowed to neither eat nor drink
until they had killed Paul.
More than forty took part in the conspiracy.
They went to the chief priests and elders
and said:
"We have bound ourselves by oath
that we will neither eat nor drink
until we have killed Paul.
It is up to you and the council
to inform the tribune
to send Paul down to you,
as though you were going to examine his case
more thoroughly.
We are prepared to dispose of him
before he reaches you."
Now the son of Paul's sister
heard of the ambush,
and he went to the fortress
and told Paul,
who called a centurion and said:
"Take this young man to the tribune,
for he has something to tell him."
So the centurion took him to the tribune
and said:
"The prisoner Paul requested
that I bring this young man to you,
for he has something to tell you."
Then the tribune took him by the hand,
drew him aside,
and asked him privately,
"What is it you have to tell me?"
He replied,
"Paul's enemies are planning to ask you
to take him down to the council tomorrow
on the pretense of examining his case.
Do not let them persuade you.
They have taken an oath
to neither eat nor drink
until they have finally killed him.
More than forty of them will ambush him.
They are waiting for word from you."

The tribune dismissed the young man
with the words,
"Tell no one you have told this to me."

◇ **Personal Reflection**

I live
so deep
inside
myself,
I seldom say
the way
I feel.
Encoded metaphors
conceal,
consoling me
as I immerse
my self
in the vast
universe.
Deep
calls to deep.
Will I find
beyond the canyons
of my mind
an echo,
flung
from afar:
I too am
the way you are.

◇ **Points for Shared Reflection**

- Do you think Paul's sister was estranged from him for disgracing the family name or was she reconciled to his conversion? Did she send her son to save her brother or did the boy go on his own? Give reasons for your replies.

- Was Paul's sister still committed to Judaism or was she a believer like Paul, either publicly or in secret? Give reasons for your reply.

- Pretend you are Paul's sister. Feel free to challenge him on his attitude toward women. You might ask him about some of his sexist statements in his letters to the churches. What are some of the concerns you would raise? What might Paul reply?

- If your sister was in serious trouble and you could not support the actions that had gotten her there, would you still stand by her? To the death? Explore the implications of this question in light of the problems families face today.

◇ **A Psalm for Those Who Are Fearful** (see p. 271)

◇ **Prayer**

O God Who Knows
the weakest link
in the chain of our becoming,
call forth the best that is in us,
which even we fail to see.
Too often we are anonymous
when it comes to the hard decisions,
unknown to others,
unknown to ourselves
when the future is on the line.
Take away our propensity
to be hesitant
and fearful,
to fashion public faces
that will mask
our personal views.
Help us stand up,
speak out,
go forth in the strength
of a thousand warriors,
yet gentle and deeply reflective
in the Spirit Who speaks
our truth.
Amen.

———— ◇ ————

◇ A PSALM FOR THOSE WHO ARE FEARFUL ◇

Choir 1   We call on You, Keeper of Courage,
to stand by us in the hard times,
to sit with us in the down times,
to walk with us in times of terror,
to give us the courage to make right choices,
choices that endanger our lives.

Choir 2   We are numbered among the fainthearted,
for we are so often fearful,
afraid to reveal our innermost thoughts,
afraid of taking chances,
afraid of speaking out for truth,
of standing up for justice,
of challenging the irresponsible,
of silencing a lie.

Choir 1   So we miss our chance at Selma
as we march behind
our protective walls,
miss our chance at networking
for systemic change,
for peace,
miss our chance for advocacy
for the homeless
and the poor,
miss the chance to say to a sister
who is black and disadvantaged:
I will take my stand with you.

Choir 2   Would we have gone to Seneca
when the sisters were convening?
Would we have joined the big parade
to push for equal rights?
Would we support a feminist
who scares us with her anger?
Would we have gone to Calvary
and remained at the foot of the cross?

Choir 1   Give us, O God, the courageous heart
of a lioness
or an eagle,
so we won't always have to deal with
what other people say,
so we won't always have to feel
the panic within us rising,
so we won't always have to struggle
to do the obvious thing.

By M. T. Winter, Crossroad Pub. Co., © 1990 Medical Mission Sisters

Choir 2   Give us the courage of Jesus
when he stood before his accusers,
when he healed the sick on the sabbath,
when he threw out the money makers
who had exploited the hallowed halls.
Give us the courage to be ourselves
in the Spirit
Who lives within us,
and may we never again be timid
when it comes to justice
and peace.

   By M. T. Winter, Crossroad Pub. Co., © 1990 Medical Mission Sisters

DRUSILLA AND BERNICE

◇ **Scripture Reference**   Acts 24:22–27
                             Acts 25:13–27; 26:1, 30–32

◇ **Biography**

Drusilla and Bernice were Jewish princesses, the daughters of Herod
Agrippa I, who, like his great grandfather Herod the Great, was king of
all Judea. The Book of Acts records that both women encountered Paul
in Caesarea while he was imprisoned there, Drusilla in the company
of her husband, Felix, the Roman procurator, and Bernice with Agrippa,
some time later, when Paul was given a provisional trial. The writer does
not mention that the women were sisters. Scripture says nothing at all
about them. It is necessary to turn to Roman historians and to the Jewish
historian Josephus in order to glean some biographical facts.

Drusilla

Drusilla was the third and youngest daughter of Agrippa I, king of Judea.
Betrothed to Epiphanes, a king's son, the marriage never took place
because he reneged on his promise to convert to Judaism. Her brother
Agrippa II arranged her marriage to Azizus, king of Amesa, who agreed
to be circumcised. When Felix was procurator of Judea, he fell in love with
Drusilla and persuaded her to leave her husband. Felix was a Gentile,
twice married, and Drusilla was still in her teens when she became his
wife. She must have been seventeen when Paul appeared before her

273

around A.D. 58. Drusilla gave birth to a son who perished in the eruption of Mount Vesuvius in A.D. 79.

Bernice

Bernice was the eldest daughter. She married the son of an Alexandrian Jewish official, and when her husband Marcus died, her father gave her in marriage to his own brother Herod. She bore him two sons before he died. During the years that followed, she was said to have had an incestuous relationship with her brother Agrippa II, with whom she appeared in Caesarea when Paul spoke in his own defense. Eventually she married Polemo, king of Cilicia, but left him shortly after and returned to Jerusalem, and it has been said, to her brother. She was in Jerusalem in A.D. 66 when the temple was ravaged and people were massacred by order of the procurator Florus. She nearly lost her life trying to prevent it. Bernice reported Florus to the proconsul, yet later when the people assembled before Agrippa, she stood with him when he urged them against any action that might lead to war. That year war did break out, and the Jews set fire to the palaces of Bernice and Agrippa. The two took an oath of allegiance to the Roman Vespasian, and Bernice became the mistress of Titus, Vespasian's son. It is said she had hoped to marry him, but he was a Roman and she was a Jew, and eventually he separated from her. She died about A.D. 79 at the age of fifty-one.

◇ **Context**

Following Paul's dramatic departure from Jerusalem, where he nearly lost his life, he arrived at Herod's palace in Caesarea, now occupied by Felix the procurator, and was imprisoned there. He met often with Felix over a period of two years, and at least one of those times, met also with Drusilla. At the end of his term, Felix was replaced, and Agrippa and Bernice came to Caesarea to welcome the new procurator. At that time, Bernice saw Paul and heard his defense. Paul was still considered a Jew, for followers of the Way were not yet seen to be a distinct religious entity, which is one reason why some Jews were so outraged at Paul's teaching and others were simply curious. Paul taught in synagogues wherever he went and took advantage of every opportunity to preach to Gentiles or Jews. His defense in Caesarea was in reality a sermon. It is not included in the lectionary reading.

◇ **Lectionary Reading**

Now Felix,
who had quite a bit of knowledge
about the Way,
adjourned the case against Paul, saying,
"When Lysias the tribune
comes to Caesarea,
I will consider your case."

He then gave orders to the centurion
that Paul be kept in custody
but be allowed some liberty,
and that none of his friends
should be prevented
from attending to his needs.
Some days later,
Felix appeared with his wife Drusilla,
who was a Jewess,
and he sent for Paul
and asked him to speak about faith
in Jesus Christ.
But when Paul preached about justice
and self-control
and the certainty of judgment,
Felix became anxious and said to Paul:
"Go away for now.
When opportunity permits,
I will send for you again."
He was also hoping for some money from Paul,
so he sent for him often
and conversed with him.
But after two years had gone by,
Felix was succeeded by Portius Festus.
Anxious to gain favor with the Jews,
Felix left Paul in prison.

Some days later,
King Agrippa and Bernice arrived in Caesarea
to greet and welcome Festus.
Their visit lasted several days,
and Festus presented Paul's case
to the king.
"There is a prisoner here
left behind by Felix.
While I was in Jerusalem,
the chief priests and elders of the Jews
submitted information about him
and demanded a sentence against him.
I said it was not our custom as Romans
to surrender a person for punishment
until the accused confronted the accusers
and was given an opportunity
to defend against the charge.
So they accompanied me here,
and the next day, without delay,

I took my seat on the tribunal
and had the man brought in.
When they were face to face,
his accusers did not charge him
with any of the crimes I had expected,
but they made some religious accusations
concerning a man named Jesus,
who supposedly is dead,
but Paul insists is still alive.
Not feeling qualified
to pass judgment on such questions,
I asked him if he would be willing
to stand trial in Jerusalem,
but he put in an appeal
for his case to be tried before the emperor,
so I am keeping him here
until I am able to send him on to Caesar."
Then Agrippa said to Festus,
"I should like to hear the man myself."
"Tomorrow you shall hear him," he replied.
The next day Agrippa and Bernice arrived
with splendid pomp and pageantry
and entered the audience hall
filled with official and prominent people.
Festus issued an order
and Paul was brought in before them.
Then Festus said to King Agrippa
and all who were assembled:
"This is the man about whom
the whole Jewish community has petitioned me,
in Jerusalem and here in Caesarea,
and they are clamoring for his death.
But from what I have learned,
he has done nothing deserving of death,
but he has appealed to Caesar,
and to Caesar he will go.
Since I have no definite charge to present
to his Imperial Majesty,
I bring him here before you now,
and especially before you, King Agrippa,
so that after we have examined him,
I will have something specific to write."
Then Agrippa said to Paul:
"You have permission to speak for yourself."
And Paul began his defense.
When he was finished, the king stood up,

and so did Bernice and the governor
and all who were sitting with them.
When they were alone
they talked together
and came to this agreement:
"This man has done nothing deserving of death
or even imprisonment."
And Agrippa remarked to Festus:
"If he had not appealed to Caesar,
this man could have gone free."

◇ **Points for Shared Reflection**

• Why is there so much biographical data for Drusilla and Bernice in contrast to the few facts available regarding other New Testament women?

• Reflect on Bernice's biography. Was she really an evil woman? Of what was she actually guilty? How does innuendo continue to shape women's reputations today?

• Incest is a horror that has ravaged many women's lives. Its power lies in the keeping of its secret and in blaming the woman who blames herself. How can we reach out to our sisters who carry such a cross? What kind of help or support should we offer?

• Why did Festus become anxious in the presence of Drusilla when Paul stopped speaking theologically and turned to issues involving behavior? Do you prefer theoretical discussion to talking about your life?

• The two male partners of the two women said they could find no fault with Paul. Would women agree with that assessment?

◇ **A Psalm Concerning False Assumptions** (see p. 278)

◇ **Prayer**
O One Who Sits upon the Throne of Truth
and judges with mercy,
make us more and more merciful,
more tolerant and more forgiving,
more able to separate fact from fiction
when according praise or blame.
Our times are replete with evil deeds,
but not all are evil-doers.
Allow us a taste of divine discernment
so we might know good from evil,
and help us be there for the victims
as a channel of Your healing grace.
Amen.

——— ◇ ———

◊ A PSALM CONCERNING FALSE ASSUMPTIONS ◊

Choir 1   Who are we to assume, O God,
the position of judge
and jury?

Choir 2   It is You Who have made the heavens
and the earth
and all who inhabit our planet.

Choir 1   It is You Who know our minds
and see through the secrecy
of our intentions.

Choir 2   It is You Who alone must scrutinize
and evaluate
who we are.

Choir 1   Who are we to accuse another
of hiding behind false motives?

Choir 2   Who are we to determine the course
of another's attitude?

Choir 1   It is You Who must name the sin,
O God,
and You Who chastise
the sinner.

Choir 2   It is You Who forgive
and reconcile
and love against the odds.

Choir 1   Deliver us from our insatiable need
to pass spontaneous judgment,
from our need to feel
that we understand
all of the pro's and con's.

Choir 2   Make us swift to forgive
and forget
and slow to show
our anger,
quick to make some excuses
for others
instead of for ourselves.

Choir 1   Deliver us from misinterpreting life
and from harboring
false assumptions,
from grossly misjudging others
on the basis of what we know.

By M. T. Winter, Crossroad Pub. Co., © 1990 Medical Mission Sisters

Choir 2   Deliver us from misunderstanding life
and from making
false accusations,
from assigning guilt
or punishment
to enemies we do not know.

Choir 1   We thank You, God, that You are a God
Who discerns the good
and the evil.

Choir 2   Wrap us around with Your goodness,
and make us more like You.

LOIS AND EUNICE

◇ **Scripture Reference**   Acts 16:1–3; 2 Timothy 1:5

◇ **Biography**

Lois was the grandmother of Timothy, Paul's trusted associate, and the mother of Eunice. Both she and Eunice, Timothy's mother, were Jewish Christians from the general area of Derbe and Lystra. Eunice was married to a Gentile, a Greek who was not a believer. The author of the second letter to Timothy praises both women for their faith, the faith as it exists within themselves and as transmitted to their offspring.

◇ **Context**

We are introduced to both women through the lens of Timothy, Paul's trusted companion. The sincerity and strength of the young man's faith, and no doubt other admirable qualities, are attributed to the influence of the women in his life. He was schooled in the tradition by his mother and his grandmother and probably learned from them the essentials of both Judaism and Christianity, for his father was neither Jew nor Christian. Timothy may have learned Jewish history but he did not follow Jewish practice, for he had to undergo circumcision before he could journey along with Paul. The women here are the ones who guarantee the faithful transmission of the Christian faith as handed down from the apostles.

Paul went to Derbe
and then on to Lystra.
There was a disciple there
named Timothy,
whose mother was a Jewish woman
who had become a believer.
His father, however, was a Greek.
Timothy was well spoken of
by the faithful at Lystra and Iconium.
Paul wanted Timothy to accompany him,
so he had him circumcised
on account of the Jews in those localities,
for they knew that his father was a Greek.

◇

I am reminded of your sincere faith,
a faith that first lived
in your grandmother Lois
and in your mother Eunice,
and now, I am sure,
lives in you.

◇ **Personal Reflection**

From my window
I can see
the twin trunks
of a towering tree,
its wide open
arms
embracing me,
a tree
of life
whose sheltering
shade
has kept
the promises
it made,
whose vibrant
green
during days
of drought
reflects
what faith
is all about.

Repository
of seeds
and song,
standing firm
through all the long
hard days
and nights
deprived of rain:
weeds
will die,
but trees
remain.
God of my childhood,
how like a tree
is deep-rooted
fidelity.

◇ **Points for Shared Reflection**

- For centuries women have been invisible, often emerging from the background only in relationship to men. Has this been true of you?

- Women often contribute significantly to the success of the men in their lives. Tell about a male family member or acquaintance who has grown because of you. What was the nature of your contribution to his growth and/or his success?

- Traditionally women transmit the faith, attend the rites, "go to church." Is this true in your family and in the church of your experience?

◇ **A Psalm in Praise of Mothers** (see p. 284)

◇ **Prayer**

We turn to You,
Shekinah-Shaddai,
when we no longer feel
we are fruitful,
when the weight that hangs
around our hearts
renders us incapable
of responding to another's need.
May the mothers of us,
the mother in us,
never cease to nurture,
for the hungers of humanity
overwhelm the limited resources
of physical motherhood,
and only the milk of the spirit
can fill the emptiness
in us all.
Mothering God,
Nurturing God,
be with us, among us, in us,
for in You we can do
miraculous things
as You make miracles
of us.
Praise be to You forever!
Amen.

――――― ◇ ―――――

◇ A PSALM IN PRAISE OF MOTHERS ◇

Leader Let us now praise mothers,
and all who are mothers of mothers.
In the name of Shaddai, our Mother,
we call blessings upon your name.

All May mercy and peace accompany you
and follow you all the way home.

Leader For all mothers who bring to birth
and contribute to God's creation:

Choir 1 For young mothers and old mothers,
first-time mothers and experienced mothers,
teenage mothers, third world mothers,
women who have contracted AIDS
and are mothers.

Choir 2 For adoptive mothers
and spiritual mothers,
and all whose love is like that of mothers,
all who give birth to ideas or music,
artistic works or any creation
that helps them think and feel like mothers,
whose creativity brings to birth in others.

All May God's creativity accompany you
and follow you all the way home.

Leader For all mothers who have lost a child,
who have suffered the pain of separation.

Choir 1 Impoverished mothers,

Choir 2 abandoned mothers,

Choir 1 mothers of suicides,

Choir 2 mothers of genocide,

Choir 1 mothers of anorexics,

Choir 2 mothers of the murdered,

Choir 1 mothers of victims of violent abuse,

Choir 2 mothers of crib death,

Choir 1 mothers of the dying,

Choir 2 mothers of the missing,

Choir 1 mothers of children slaughtered in war,

Choir 2 mothers of children slain in the streets,

Choir 1 mothers of kidnapped children,

Choir 2 mothers of children who are in prison,

 By M. T. Winter, Crossroad Pub. Co., © 1990 Medical Mission Sisters

Choir 1	mothers of children who are criminally insane,
Choir 2	mothers of children who ran away from home,
Choir 1	mothers whose children will never come home,
Choir 2	mothers whose home has never had children,
All	May God's comfort accompany you and follow you all the way home.
Leader	For all mothers who reach out to other people, who nurture and feed the world.

Choir 1 For mothers in leadership positions:
- in public life
- in business
- in academic institutions
- in the arts and communication
- in religion
- in the church

Choir 2 For mothers who are behind the scenes:
- at home with the family
- in service jobs
- in voluntary organizations
- in household industries
- in religion
- in the church

All	May the Spirit of God empower you and follow you all the way home.
Leader	May Shaddai, our Mother, bless all mothers.
All	Thank you, Shaddai, for all our mothers. May their spirit inspire forever.

By M. T. Winter, Crossroad Pub. Co., © 1990 Medical Mission Sisters

ELECT LADY

◇ **Scripture Reference**   2 John 1–13

◇ **Biography**

The elect lady (*eklektē kyria*) to whom the second letter of John was directed is not considered to be a historical figure by most biblical scholars, who conclude that the enigmatic title signifies an unknown congregation addressed in the symbolic language of the Johannine writer. Although internal evidence favors such a collective symbol, some scholars past and present have supported the theory of an individual. Assuming she did exist, she was a woman who remains anonymous to us, and as such, she symbolizes the multitude of unidentified, unacknowledged women who have contributed to the life of the church.

◇ **Context**

In the years following the death and resurrection of Jesus, many women were part of the circle of leadership whose preaching, teaching, and apostolic activities contributed to the spread of Christianity through the establishment of local church communities. As time passed, an inherent patriarchy with its penchant for uniformity and control led to a significant reordering of church life. When there was no longer anyone alive who remembered the way it really was with Jesus, orthodoxy came on with a vengeance and female leadership, once acceptable, became improbable and, eventually, unthinkable.

The elect lady of the Johannine letter may well have been a female leader of a house church at the end of an era when such leadership, once prevalent, had all but disappeared. When heretical influences were splitting the church, Johannine communities were often at the core of the controversy. False teaching failed to acknowledge that the Christ was indeed incarnate in the humanity of Jesus. Was the letter writer's warning issued to a community or to its leader? The tendency to describe the church in terms of female imagery eventually became the norm within Christian tradition. The determination to rid the church of every trace of female equality also prevailed.

Nevertheless, Clement of Alexandria (ca. 200) wrote that the second letter of John was addressed "to a certain Babylonian woman named 'Electa,' which signifies the election of the holy church." Athanasius (ca. 340) saw *Kyria* as a personal name and suggested "the noble Kyria" as the one who was addressed. Some contemporary scholars agree that an individual woman was meant and that *kyria*, like *domina* (Latin for "Lady"), was a term of courtesy, concluding that the letter was written to an unnamed female of some significance in one of the churches of Asia Minor. Therefore, a legitimate case can be made for the historical validity of the elect lady, particularly in light of recent feminist awareness of the many female church leaders previously thought not to exist.

Whether the "elect" or "chosen of God" was a congregation or a woman may never be fully determined, but we do know that when women leaders were no longer visible in the church, they were highly visible as priests and prophets in communities outside of orthodox Christianity. The elect lady may well have been one of the last female leaders of a local community in an increasingly orthodox church sometime around the close of the turbulent first century of the Christian era.

◇ **Lectionary Reading**

From the elder to the elect lady,
the chosen one,
and to her children,
whom I love in the truth,
not only I
but also all who know the truth
which is in us
and with us forever:
Grace, mercy, and peace
will be with us
from God our Creator
and Jesus, God's Child
in truth and love.
It has given me great joy
to find that your children
have been living the life of truth,

just as God has commanded.
I write to you now, dear lady,
not to give you a new commandment,
but the one we have had from the beginning,
and to plead:
let us love one another.
To love is to live
according to the law
of love
which you have heard
from the beginning:
to live a life of love.
For many deceivers have entered the world
who refuse to acknowledge
that Jesus Christ has come
in the flesh.
They are the Deceiver,
the Antichrist.
Be careful, that you may not lose
what you have worked for,
but may receive the reward you deserve.
Anyone who goes beyond the teaching of Christ
does not have God within them.
Only those who keep to what Christ has taught
have both the Creator and Christ.
Whoever comes with a different doctrine
must not be received in your house,
or even be given a greeting.
If you greet them,
you share in their wicked work.
There are things I have to tell you,
but I would rather not do this
with paper and ink.
Instead, I hope to come to see you
and talk with you face to face,
so that our joy may be complete.
The children of your elect sister
greet you.

◇ **Personal Reflection**

The delicate fronds
of a coconut palm
keep the tropical sun
from burning
the lone
stone white

observers
of an ancient
liturgy:
the long
lean line
their backs bent
to the pull
of the tide
moves
hand
over hand
over centuries
of sweat
and a strong
surf song,
heaves
retrieves
slowly
oh, so slowly
the net
eternally returning
with treasures
from the sea,
as the rite
ensures
that these few fish
will feed
all
who hunger
for self-sufficiency.

⋄ **Points for Shared Reflection**

• Consider this biblical letter within its contextual setting. Who do you think the elect lady was, and on what facts do you base your opinion? Who was her elect sister to whom the letter's last line refers?

• A lot has been written about the theological controversies of this period of church development. How might the church's increasingly restrictive attitude toward women have contributed to the crisis?

• The disappearance of women from leadership positions within the church coincided with the rise of other expressions of Christianity and of women leaders within those groups. What relationship do you see between that period of church history and our own?

• Would you agree that the church has helped foster some of the heresies it condemns? If so, give examples that support your view.

• Why is the history always "his" and the heresy always "hers"?

◇ **A Psalm in Times of Trial** (see p. 291)

◇ **Prayer**

O Blessed Priority,
help us to choose You
above all else,
whatever the implications,
for all other choice
is peripheral
to the Choice Who
chooses us.
You are the taproot
of the spirit,
in You the heart takes wing,
for only You
in times of trial
can make the silence
sing.
Amen.

——— ◇ ———

◇ A PSALM IN TIMES OF TRIAL ◇

Choir 1   How shall I stand if I stand alone
when everything goes against me,
when the ground
once firm beneath my feet
has the feel of shifting sand?

Choir 2   What do I say when the ones I trust
cross examine my inspiration,
when the God of my heart
no longer fits
the old theological frame?

Choir 1   Who lives by faith
cannot evade
the fact of a crucifixion,
cannot escape
the inevitable sting
of the nails
or the lash
or the lance.

Choir 2   Hope cannot rise
until one dies
completely
in soul and spirit,
feels absolute abandonment
and knows the night
of the tomb.

Choir 1   Who can survive
irretrievable loss?
The kind that cuts the heart in half,
dashes the senses against the rocks,
smashes the will to go on giving,
ending forever
the way we were.

Choir 2   Who among us has not mourned the loss
of childhood's imaginary friend,
the end of a cherished relationship,
the moving beyond the perimeters
of our own securities,
the death of the God
of our own making?

Choir 1   Myths crumble, boxes break,
Mystery bursts
beyond our boundaries,

By M. T. Winter, Crossroad Pub. Co., © 1990 Medical Mission Sisters   *WomanWord* / **291**

refuses to fit
our frames of reference,
refuses to leave us,
will not leave us,
even as structures
no longer serve us,
oldtime religion
no longer saves us.

Choir 2   O Mystery, You are beyond
the borders of our best intentions,
there at the point
of unbearable pain,
at the root
of every small hope
rising,
the Center
entering,
centering
all.

Choir 1   You make a way
where there is no way,
You teach us
to walk on water,
to pick up the broken remnants
of our shattered expectations
and begin to build
again.

Choir 2   You give the words
we are to say
in times of trial
or temptation,
and you give the strength
to walk away
when we cannot overcome.

Choir 1   Blessed Assurance,
be with us always,
let Your grace
enfold us.

Choir 2   Peaceful Persuasion,
stay with us
to heal us
and to hold us.

   By M. T. Winter, Crossroad Pub. Co., © 1990 Medical Mission Sisters

WOMEN IN THE CHURCH

◇ **Scripture Reference**   Acts 5:12–14; 8:3; 9:1–2; 22:4–7
                                        Acts 6:1; 8:5, 12; 17:1–4, 12
                                        1 Corinthians 9:5 / Galatians 3:27–28
                                        1 Corinthians 7:13–16; 11:5; 14:35–36
                                        1 Timothy 5:5, 9–10

◇ **Biography**

Women who were touched, healed, and forgiven by Jesus, women disciples who accompanied Jesus, remained with him when he died, witnessed his resurrection and received his Holy Spirit, family members of apostles and disciples, all of these women formed the first female nucleus of the New Testament church which quickly spread beyond Judea, Galilee, and Samaria into Asia Minor, Greece, and Rome. Some of these women we know by name; most remain anonymous. They were the poor, the wealthy, and the widows, women of nobility and of low social status, even slaves, married and unmarried, wives of believers and wives of unbelievers. Among them were house church leaders, missionaries, and co-workers with Paul in a ministry of evangelization and teaching. Among them were apostolic eyewitnesses, empowered by their visionary-ecstatic experiences to expand the Jesus movement whose Sophia-God made possible their participation in a discipleship of equals.

◇ **Context**

The scriptural records of early church experience were written from a later perspective by male writers and redactors who reflect a developing orthodoxy and a patriarchal bias. Elisabeth Schüssler Fiorenza tells us that these written records must be read as androcentric texts and approached with a hermeneutics of suspicion as we struggle to clarify what is the word of God for us among the many words of men. A growing number of feminist scholars conclude that scripture texts which subordinate and exclude no longer function as revelation for women because true Gospel liberates, it does not enslave.

While all the texts pertaining to historical women in the New Testament are in this lectionary collection, not every passage containing male advice to female church members appears here. Deutero-Pauline and even some Pauline passages which pertain to women's behavior have been edited or eliminated as seemingly unfair both to women and to God, and in some instances, even to Paul. However, some texts which demean women have been included because they bear witness to some very important fact of women's participation, such as the textual evidence concerning women's prophesying or their speaking out in the church, a fact at the heart of Paul's injunction for them to keep silent. These texts have been included for information and discussion and not as proclamation.

Texts that attest to the growth of female membership and the historical fact of their persecution, texts that support women's presence and participation, that contribute to a sense of women's history and women's worth or to their struggle to remain equal within a patriarchal milieu, these constitute the lectionary reading. This final consideration of all women in the New Testament church must be seen and celebrated in the context of all that we have learned from our previous reflections on the lives of individual women, whose lections are not repeated here.

◇ **Lectionary Reading**

They used to meet together
in the Portico of Solomon.
No one else dared to join them,
although they were well respected.
So many signs and wonders

were worked among the people
at the hands of the apostles
that more and more were added
to the community of believers,
multitudes of women
and multitudes of men.

◇

Saul set out to destroy the church.
He went from house to house,
arresting women
as well as men,
and had them put in prison.

◇

Threatening to slaughter
the disciples of the Christ,
Saul went to the high priest
and asked for letters
addressed to the synagogues in Damascus,
authorizing him to arrest
any women or men
who were followers of the Way,
so that he might bring them
to Jerusalem.

◇

"I persecuted this Way to the death,
and sent women
as well as men
to prison in chains,
as the high priest
and the councils of elders
can attest,
since they sent me with letters
to Damascus.
I intended to take prisoners
back to Jerusalem
so that they might be punished.
During that journey,
around midday,
as I drew near to Damascus,
a heavenly light suddenly shone around me.
I fell to the ground

and I heard a voice saying,
'Saul, Saul, why do you persecute me?' "

◇

When the number of disciples
was increasing,
the Hellenists complained
about the Hebrews
because their widows
were neglected
in the daily distribution.

◇

Philip went to a town of Samaria
and proclaimed the Christ to them.
When they believed the good news
Philip preached
about the reign of God
and the name of Jesus Christ,
they were baptized,
both women and men.

◇

They passed through Amphipolis
and Apollonia
and came to Thessalonica.
According to his custom,
Paul attended the synagogue there.
For three consecutive sabbaths,
they debated the scriptures
as Paul explained
how the Christ had to suffer
and rise from the dead.
"This Jesus Whom I proclaim to you,
he is the Christ," Paul insisted.
Some of them were persuaded
and they joined Paul and Silas.
So did many devout Greeks
and quite a few of the leading women.

◇

In Borea many Jews became believers.
So did many upper-class women from among the Greeks,
as well as a number of men.

◇

Do we not have the right
to be accompanied by a sister,
or a wife,
like all the other apostles
and the brothers of Jesus
and Cephas?

◇

All who are baptized in Christ
are clothed in Christ,
and now there is
neither Jew nor Greek,
neither slave nor free,
there is no male and female,
for all are one in Christ Jesus.

◇ **For Discussion Only (Optional)**

If a believer has a wife
who is an unbeliever,
and she is content to live with him,
her husband must not send her away;
and if a woman is married to an unbeliever,
and he agrees to remain with her,
she is not to leave him.
For the unbelieving husband
is made one with the saints
through his wife,
and the unbelieving wife
is made one with the saints
through her husband,
otherwise your children
would be unclean,
but as it is,
they are holy.
However, if the unbelieving partner
prefers to separate, they may.
In a situation such as this,
the sister or the brother
is not bound,
for God has called you to a life of peace.
If you are a wife,
it may well be that it is your role
to save your husband,

and if you are a husband,
it may be up to you to save your wife.

◇

If a woman prays or prophesies
with her head unveiled,
it is as if she had shaved off her hair.

◇

It does not seem right for a woman
to speak out in the church.
Do you think the word of God
originated with you?
Or that it has come only to you?

◇

A woman who is truly widowed,
and is left all alone,
can dedicate herself to God
and continue day and night
with petitions and prayers.
Enrollment as a widow is permissible
for a woman at least sixty years of age
who has had only one husband.
She must be known for her good works
and for the way she has raised her children,
shown hospitality to strangers,
washed the feet of the saints,
helped people who are in trouble,
and she must be devoted to doing good.

◇ **Personal Reflection**

God
by any other name
is God
omnipotent
all the same.
There are many paths
through the forest,
some of them
unknown.
We travel together
in company
or make our way
alone.

Some move
through muddy waters,
others walk
dry shod,
each of us
seeking
an avenue
into the heart
of God.

⋄ **Points for Shared Reflection**

- Women in the early centuries of Christianity endured persecution both outside and inside the church. Give instances of how this is also true of the church of our day?

- Many women remained within the church even as their roles shifted from active involvement to a passive presence. Today the majority of church members are female. Why are so many women attracted to and loyal to the church? Why are you?

- Today's women-church, like the Jesus movement and the early Christian missionary movement, is less institutional and more charismatically inclusive. Are you attracted to this kind of religious phenomenon? If so, why? If not, why not?

- Now that you have seen and celebrated the evidence of women's active involvement in the leadership and life of the early church, what impact will this have on your own participation? What are your hopes for women in the church of the future? What will you do to help ensure the fulfillment of these hopes?

⋄ **A Psalm for All God's People** (see p. 301)

◇ **Prayer**

To You we lift our songs of praise,
O Sacred Sound of Silence,
as we seek You in the wisdom of ages
and speak to You those secrets
we simply could not, would not share.
You weave of the earth,
of all people on earth
a tapestry of benediction,
creating patterns
of possible peace,
untangling our justice efforts,
securing our separate strands of hope
into an integrated vision
of homespun spirit
and Spirit ways.
Call us forth and consecrate us
to a service of self-surrender.
Our lives, our loves,
are in Your hands,
now and forever.
Amen.

———— ◇ ————

◇ A PSALM FOR ALL GOD'S PEOPLE ◇

Choir 1   We thank You, O Creator God,
for making us all Your people,

Choir 2   for inviting all Your children
into the household of liberty.

Choir 1   You created us weak
yet make us strong
in the power
of Your Spirit.

Choir 2   You sustain us
as we live by faith:
holy is Your name.

Choir 1   You made us equal,
female and male,
and for this
all women are grateful.

Choir 2   There is nothing now
that can separate us
from the Christa
Who is our God.

Choir 1   You are there for us,
Sophia Shaddai,
when our hearts cry out
for wisdom
and our spirits search
for comfort.

Choir 2   You weave a web of security
from the tangled threads
of terror
that invade us
when we are vulnerable
and stomp on us
when we are down.

Choir 1   Though winds whistle
within
and sudden storms break
all around us,
gentle
is Your presence.

Choir 2   In the midst of our frustration,
You devise
simple solutions

By M. T. Winter, Crossroad Pub. Co., © 1990 Medical Mission Sisters

to the complexities
that abound.

Choir 1   You settle us down
when our rage erupts,
spilling words
or silence
on the hearts of those
we cherish,

Choir 2   and You call our best selves
to life again
to redeem us
and to prepare the way
for us to forgive
ourselves.

Choir 1   You take control
when we are out of control,
during all those times
when we cannot control
the evil
affecting the lives
of those
who look to us
for protection,

Choir 2   and when insidious persecution
persists,
You cover our soft
underbelly
of feeling
with an invincible
shield.

Choir 1   You fill us with peace
as You hold us close,
O Center and Source
of our loving,
making a space
for Your sensitive ones
in Your everlasting arms.

Choir 2   You are the Word beyond
our words
when we ache to say
I love you,
and You love us
into remembering

    By M. T. Winter, Crossroad Pub. Co., © 1990 Medical Mission Sisters

not what we want
but what You will.

Choir 1   Weave of our lives, O Weaver God,
a tapestry
of salvation;
may the thin threads
of our deficiencies
add a texture
of grateful praise.

Choir 2   Mold us like clay in the hands
of a potter,
to a shape
as yet unimagined
and a future
as yet undefined.

Choir 1   O Sacred Trust, we entrust to You
all that we have
or hope
or hallow.

Choir 2   In You we are a people,
with You
we have a purpose,
through You
we have potential
to redeem and renew
our times.

Choir 1   Help us to hear the unspoken cries
of the desperately poor
in our cities.

Choir 2   Help us to stand together
with the underside
of society
and the outcasts
of the world.

Choir 1   Help us to lift each other up
when the going gets tough
and we get discouraged
because justice is
so slow.

Choir 2   Help us to be world citizens
committed
to global freedom
and to helping people
grow.

By M. T. Winter, Crossroad Pub. Co., © 1990 Medical Mission Sisters

Women bear
the waters of life....

◇ A PSALM OF UNITY AMONG WOMEN OF FAITH ◇

Leader   How good it is when women of faith
are bonded together in unity,
when sisters reach out to sisters,
when women of the present learn
from women of the past.
Let us name our sister pioneers.
Let us claim our sister saints.

All   Elizabeth our sister,
how good it is to name you:

Choir 1   teach us to grow old gracefully.

All   Mary, mother of Jesus, our sister,
how good it is to name you:

Choir 2   teach us to risk all without regret.

All   Anna our sister,
how good it is to name you:

Choir 1   help us to trust our inner wisdom.

All   Joanna our sister,
how good it is to name you:

Choir 2   inspire us to discipleship.

All   Susanna our sister,
how good it is to name you:

Choir 1   show us how to follow Jesus.

All   Mary, mother of James and Joseph, our sister,
how good it is to name you:

Choir 2   help us to be steadfast in the face of pain and death.

All   Mary, mother of John Mark, our sister,
how good it is to name you:

Choir 1   may people feel at home with us
as they felt at home with you.

All   Mary, wife of Cleopas, our sister,
how good it is to name you:

Choir 2   help us to recognize Jesus in the broken lives
of the poor.

All   Mary of Bethany, our sister,
how good it is to name you:

Choir 1   help us to be friends with Jesus.

By M. T. Winter, Crossroad Pub. Co., © 1990 Medical Mission Sisters   *WomanWord* / **305**

All	Mary of Magdala, our sister, how good it is to name you:
Choir 2	help us witness to the risen Christ.
All	Mary of Rome, our sister, how good it is to name you:
Choir 1	may your experience in ministry give validity to our call.
All	Martha of Bethany, our sister, how good it is to name you:
Choir 2	your energy and hospitality are an example to us all.
All	Salome, wife of Zebedee, our sister, how good it is to name you:
Choir 1	you give us courage to speak out.
All	Dorcas our sister, how good it is to name you:
Choir 2	through you our dreams of equality come to life again.
All	Rhoda our sister, how good it is to name you:
Choir 1	support our spontaneity.
All	Lydia our sister, how good it is to name you:
Choir 2	like you we are called to minister in the church and in the world.
All	Damaris our sister, how good it is to name you:
Choir 1	like you we are open to new ways of being in the world.
All	Euodia our sister, how good it is to name you:
Choir 2	because we too have felt alienated, we can identify with you.
All	Syntyche our sister, how good it is to name you:
Choir 1	your struggle with relationship is a struggle we have known.
All	Phoebe our sister, how good it is to name you:
Choir 2	the silence surrounding your significance seals our sisterhood.

                    By M. T. Winter, Crossroad Pub. Co., © 1990 Medical Mission Sisters

All	Prisca our sister, how good it is to name you:
Choir 1	your witness to having both marriage and ministry is a symbol of hope for us.
All	Julia our sister, how good it is to name you:
Choir 2	we are encouraged by your ministry in Rome.
All	Junia our sister, how good it is to name you:
Choir 1	we are inspired by your ministry in Rome.
All	Tryphena our sister, how good it is to name you:
Choir 2	we are strengthened by your ministry in Rome.
All	Tryphosa our sister, how good it is to name you:
Choir 1	we are energized by your ministry in Rome.
All	Persis our sister, how good it is to name you:
Choir 2	we are empowered by your ministry in Rome.
All	Nympha our sister, how good it is to name you:
Choir 1	our spirit reaches out to yours.
All	Apphia our sister, how good it is to name you:
Choir 2	intercede for us.
All	Chloe our sister, how good it is to name you:
Choir 1	bring peace to our troubled hearts.
All	Claudia our sister, how good it is to name you:
Choir 2	guide our search for meaning.
All	Lois our sister, how good it is to name you:
Choir 1	strengthen us in faith.
All	Eunice our sister, how good it is to name you:
Choir 2	help us hold fast to hope.

All	Herodias our sister, we name you and we claim you:
Choir 1	for you are one of us.
All	Salome, daughter of Herodias, our sister, we name you and we claim you:
Choir 2	you too are one of us.
All	Sapphira our sister, we name you and we claim you:
Choir 1	the truth of your experience is not yet known to us.
All	Drusilla our sister, we name you and we claim you:
Choir 2	although your ways are strange to us.
All	Bernice our sister, we name you and we claim you:
Choir 1	your pain is a part of us.
All	Peter's mother-in-law, our sister, how good it is to claim you:
Choir 2	may our service to others also follow a healing within ourselves.
All	Woman accused of adultery, our sister, how good it is to claim you:
Choir 1	help those among us who have been abused find strength to begin again.
All	Woman who anointed Jesus' feet, our sister, how good it is to claim you:
Choir 2	help us not to doubt ourselves when we are wrongly accused.
All	Woman who anointed Jesus' head, our sister, how good it is to claim you:
Choir 1	help us to be faithful to what God reveals.
All	Widow of Nain, our sister, how good it is to claim you:
Choir 2	be one with us in our sense of loss.
All	Woman with the flow of blood, our sister, how good it is to claim you:
Choir 1	help us to be truly female in all we say and do.
All	Jairus's daughter, our sister, how good it is to claim you:
Choir 2	help us raise to life the little girl asleep in us.

   By M. T. Winter, Crossroad Pub. Co., © 1990 Medical Mission Sisters

All	Crippled woman, our sister, how good it is to claim you:
Choir 1	help us overcome the discrimination crippling us.
All	Poor widow, our sister, how good it is to claim you:
Choir 2	help us to share what we have and are with those who are deprived.
All	Canaanite woman, our sister, how good it is to claim you:
Choir 1	may we too have the tenacity to push for miracles.
All	Canaanite woman's daughter, our sister, how good it is to claim you:
Choir 2	be a friend and counselor to all our troubled daughters.
All	Woman in the crowd, our sister, how good it is to claim you:
Choir 1	we too would proclaim what we see and know.
All	Woman at the well, our sister, how good it is to claim you:
Choir 2	help us to worship in spirit and in truth.
All	Pilate's wife, our sister, how good it is to claim you:
Choir 1	you teach us to trust our intuition.
All	High priest's maid, our sister, how good it is to claim you:
Choir 2	help us to deal with denial regarding the truth of who we are.
All	Mary's sister, our sister, how good it is to claim you:
Choir 1	help us to know your sister as a woman and a friend.
All	Sisters of Jesus, our sisters, how good it is to claim you:
Choir 2	help us to know and love your brother unconditionally.
All	Daughters of Jerusalem, our sisters, how good it is to claim you:
Choir 1	continue to weep for us.
All	Women who accompanied Jesus, our sisters, how good it is to claim you:
Choir 2	support us in our struggle to follow Jesus today.

By M. T. Winter, Crossroad Pub. Co., © 1990 Medical Mission Sisters   *WomanWord* / **309**

All	Women at Pentecost, our sisters, how good it is to claim you:
Choir 1	you confirm that the Spirit speaks through women.
All	Philip's four prophetic daughters, our sisters, how good it is to claim you:
Choir 2	speak to us and through us your bold prophetic word.
All	Female slave of Philippi, our sister, how good it is to claim you:
Choir 1	teach us the ways of wisdom known to women long ago.
All	Paul's sister, our sister, how good it is to claim you:
Choir 2	how can we demythologize your brother so that women might have their say?
All	Sister of Nereus, our sister, how good it is to claim you:
Choir 1	help all anonymous women to claim their identity.
All	Mother of Rufus, our sister, how good it is to claim you:
Choir 2	encourage all mothers to name and claim their ministry.
All	Elect lady, our sister, how good it is to claim you:
Choir 1	we too will be priests and bishops in memory of you.
All	All women in the church, our sisters, how good it is to claim you:
Choir 2	for you are our tradition of prophets, disciples, ministers,
All	the first of a cloud of witnesses to the work of the Holy Spirit through the women of Christianity. We thank you for your faithfulness. You are role models for us all.

 By M. T. Winter, Crossroad Pub. Co., © 1990 Medical Mission Sisters

◇ **SONGS** ◇

WELLSPRINGS OF WOMEN

Wellsprings of women, rise and bless
the Source of our resourcefulness.
We come together to confess
our need to know we're Wisdom's daughters
and to quench our thirst for living waters.

Wellsprings of women, wise ones weep
for promises we've yet to keep.
Still waters still, our doubts run deep,
while gifts of God within are growing
like a fountain, full to overflowing.

Wellsprings of women, born to be
a paradigm of liberty,
the hope of all who would be free
to sail the seas in search of healing,
all the while the ways of Love revealing.

Wellsprings of women, this day brings
the silent strength of hidden springs,
the news of which creation sings:
the tears we shed, the themes we're stressing
wash the wounds of earth and bring a blessing.

    By M. T. Winter, Crossroad Pub. Co., © 1990 Medical Mission Sisters

WELLSPRINGS OF WOMEN

*Words and Music by
Miriam Therese Winter*

1. Well - springs of wom - en, rise and bless the Source of our re - source - ful - ness. We come to - geth - er to con - fess our need to know we're Wis - dom's daugh - ters and to quench our thirst for liv - ing wa - ters.

2. Well - springs of wom - en, wise ones weep for prom - is - es we've yet to keep; still wa - ters still, our doubts run deep while gifts of God with - in are grow - ing like a foun - tain, full to o - ver - flow - ing.

3. Well - springs of wom - en, born to be a par - a - digm of lib - er - ty, the hope of all who would be free to sail the seas in search of heal - ing, all the while the ways of Love re - veal - ing.

4. Well - springs of wom - en, this day brings the si - lent strength of hid - den springs, the news of which cre - a - tion sings: the tears we shed, the themes we're stress - ing wash the wounds of earth and bring a bless - ing.

Copyright © Medical Mission Sisters, 1987, 1990

HOLY THE NEW DAY

Holy the New Day about to break,
when all the walled up wisdom will suddenly awake,
when liberty and harmony erase our global pain,
when none on earth need ever take up arms again,
when all will hear and understand
the still, small voice of grace,
when all who seek will see the Holy Face
of Mystery, Unity, and cry:
Holy the Day of Shaddai.

Holy the New Age we bring to birth,
when we are one with everyone who cherishes the earth,
when gentleness and tenderness are hallmarks of the strong,
when peace and justice are the substance of our song,
when deep within the heart of you
there is a part of me,
when all will grow to know that they are free.
O Mystery, Unity, we cry:
Holy the Age of Shaddai.
Holy, Holy, Shaddai.

    By M. T. Winter, Crossroad Pub. Co., © 1987 Medical Mission Sisters

HOLY THE NEW DAY

Words and Music by
Miriam Therese Winter

Ho - ly _____ the New Day a - bout to
Ho - ly _____ the New Age we bring to

break, _____ when all the walled up wis - dom will _____ sud - den - ly a -
birth, _____ when we are one with ev - 'ry - one who _____ cher - ish - es the

wake, _____ when _____ lib - er - ty and har - mo - ny e - rase our glo - bal
earth, _____ when _____ gen - tle - ness and ten - der - ness are hall - marks of the

pain, when none on earth need ev - er take up arms a - gain, when
strong, when peace and jus - tice are the sub - stance of our song, when

all will hear and un - der - stand the still, small voice of grace, when all who
deep with - in the heart of you there is a part of me, when all will

seek will see the Ho - ly Face of Mys - ter - y, _____
grow to know that they are free. O Mys - ter - y, _____

U - ni - ty, _____ and cry: Ho - ly the Day of Shad -
U - ni - ty, _____ we cry: Ho - ly the Age of Shad -

1. dai.
2. dai.

Ho - ly, Ho - ly, Shad - dai.

GOD OF MY CHILDHOOD

God of my childhood and my call,
make me a window, not a wall.
So like an icon, may I be
a sign of love's transparency,
and through the love that lives in me,
proclaim Your lasting love for all.

Come, O my Maker, make of me
a mirror, so that all may see
within themselves, Your saving grace,
reflection of Your Holy Face,
an image of Your warm embrace
and nurturing Reality.

Creator, recreate us all.
Come, lift us up before we fall.
You are the Wisdom and the Way,
the Dawning of Unending Day,
the Word we sometimes fail to say
within our canon of recall.

God of our future, help us see
a vision of the yet-to-be:
in You is freedom from our fears,
a silent strength and no more tears;
in You dissension disappears
into a global harmony.

God of all gods, to You we sing
a song of Your imagining:
a liberating melody,
to set our shackled spirits free,
to tell us that Your canopy
of care is all-encompassing.

 By M. T. Winter, Crossroad Pub. Co., © 1990 Medical Mission Sisters

GOD OF MY CHILDHOOD

*Words and Music by
Miriam Therese Winter*

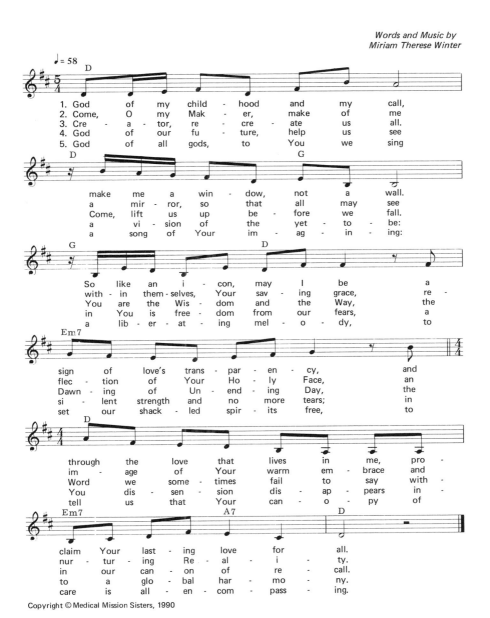

1. God of my child - hood and my call,
2. Come, O my Mak - er, make of me
3. Cre - a - tor, re - cre - ate us all.
4. God of our fu - ture, help us see
5. God of all gods, to You we sing

make me a win - dow, not a wall.
a mir - ror, so that all may see
Come, lift us up be - fore we fall.
a vi - sion of the yet - to - be:
a song of Your im - ag - in - ing:

So like an i - con, may I be a
with - in them - selves, Your sav - ing grace, re -
You are the Wis - dom and the Way, the
in You is free - dom from our fears, a
a lib - er - at - ing mel - o - dy, to

sign of love's trans - par - en - cy, and
flec - tion of Your Ho - ly Face, an
Dawn - ing of Un - end - ing Day, the
si - lent strength and no more tears; in
set our shack - led spir - its free, to

through the love that lives in me, pro -
im - age of Your warm em - brace and
Word we some - times fail to say with -
You dis - sen - sion dis - ap - pears in -
tell us that Your can - o - py of

claim Your last - ing love for all.
nur - tur - ing Re - al - i - ty.
in our can - on of re - call.
to a glo - bal har - mo - ny.
care is all - en - com - pass - ing.

O FOR A WORLD

O for a world where everyone
respects each other's ways,
where love is lived and all is done
with justice and with praise.

O for a world where goods are shared
and misery relieved,
where truth is spoken, children spared,
equality achieved.

We welcome one world family
and struggle with each choice
that opens us to unity
and gives our vision voice.

The poor are rich, the weak are strong,
the foolish ones are wise.
Tell all who mourn, outcasts belong,
who perishes will rise.

O for a world preparing for
God's glorious reign of peace,
where time and tears will be no more,
and all but love will cease.

     By M. T. Winter, Crossroad Pub. Co., © 1990 Medical Mission Sisters

O FOR A WORLD

Words by
Miriam Therese Winter

Music by
Carl Gotthelf Gläser, 1828

1. O for a world where ev - ery - one re -
2. O for a world where goods are shared and
3. We wel - come one world fam - i - ly and
4. The poor are rich, the weak are strong, the
5. O for a world pre - par - ing for God's

spects each oth - er's ways, where love is lived and
mis - er - y re - lieved, where truth is spo - ken,
strug - gle with each choice that o - pens us to
fool - ish ones are wise. Tell all who mourn: out -
glo - rious reign of peace, where time and tears will

all is done with jus - tice and with praise.
chil - dren spared, e - qual - i - ty a - chieved.
u - ni - ty and who per - ish - es will voice.
casts be - long, who per - ish - es will rise.
be no more, and all but love will cease.